The Gathering Place *for* Making Memories

The Christmas Kitchen

Tammy Maltby *with*
Anne Christian Buchanan

HOWARD BOOKS
A DIVISION OF SIMON & SCHUSTER
New York   London   Toronto   Sydney

Our purpose at Howard Books is to:

- Increase faith in the hearts of growing Christians
- Inspire holiness in the lives of believers
- Instill hope in the hearts of struggling people everywhere

Because He's coming again!

Published by Howard Books, a division of Simon & Schuster, Inc.
1230 Avenue of the Americas, New York, NY 10020
www.howardpublishing.com

The Christmas Kitchen © 2009 by Tammy Maltby and Anne Christian Buchanan

In association with Bill Jensen and William K. Jensen Literary Services

Library of Congress Control Number:2009003228

ISBN 978-1-4165-8765-1

10 9 8 7 6 5 4 3 2 1

Manufactured in China

For information regarding special discounts for bulk purchases, please contact:
Simon & Schuster Special Sales at 1-866-506-1949 or business@simonandschuster.com.

Edited by Between the Lines
Cover and Interior design by Thinkpen Design, Inc., www.thinkpendesign.com
Photo Credits
Jupiter Images Unlimited: pp. 6, 14, 25, 26, 34, 35, 36, 46, 56, 68, 86, 98, 108, 122;
iStockphoto: p. 12; Shutterstock: pp. 61, 63, 64, 67, 112, 113, 114, 126, 127
All other photos are courtesy of the author.

Contents

Contents

To Bill

for the title, for the inspiration,
but most of all for the friendship

Chapter 1

Christmas Central

The key to making your holiday dreams come true

In so many ways, the kitchen is the heart of the home. And when the holidays roll around, the kitchen is—or should be—Christmas Central.

The kitchen is where so many Christmas memories come from, where so many Christmas dreams begin. It's a place of intoxicating aromas, tantalizing tastes—of bustling activity and endless creativity. It's a place where old meets new, where tradition gets spiced up with fresh ideas, where grown-ups and kids, friends and family, come to together to cook and prepare and enjoy the festive results.

You know what I'm talking about. There's the spicy-sweet, familiar fragrance of cinnamon and apples, the tangy taste of cranberries and cider, the sugary goodness of Christmas cookies. There's the childlike fun of playing with flour and sugar, the reward of giving presents you've made with your own hands. There's the camaraderie of swapping stories while chopping onions, the creative satisfaction of setting a beautiful table and gathering friends and acquaintances for a festive party. And of course there's the joy of gathering around a table to celebrate the coming of Love into the world.

All these things are what the Christmas Kitchen means to me, to most of us. And I'm not just talking about the kitchen at Grandma's house or in a Norman Rockwell fantasy or on the pages of your gorgeous coffee-table Christmas book. I believe any kitchen can be the place where the fun and heartwarming business of Christmas memory making begins. And I promise you, you don't have to be June Cleaver or Martha Stewart—or even Tammy Maltby—to pull it off.

Your kitchen, whatever it looks like, is your number one resource for holiday celebration and decoration. It's your comforting place to nurture relationships with people related by blood and those you choose to welcome into your life. It's rich with possibilities for gift giving, for expressing thanks, for reaching out to others and showing love to them. It's also an ideal place to connect with children, passing along the experience of Christmas and recovering a little of the child in you at the same time.

Or it *can* be all those things—if you don't let the busyness of the season or your own inflated expectations or kitchen insecurities overwhelm you.

But that's the problem, isn't it? So many women I know long to have the kind of delicious, fragrant, fun, and festive holiday I've just described. They pore over magazines, delighting in the beautiful images and ideas. But that stuff doesn't happen in their own homes—not the way they'd hoped. And they cite any number of reasons.

"My kitchen (or my house) is too small."

"I'm not much of a cook."

"The idea of entertaining scares me to death."

"The kids are too small—they're all underfoot."

"The kids are all grown—why bother?"

"I don't have kids—I don't even have a family!"

"Money's tight."

And then there's the perennial "I'm just too busy!"

We're all too busy—with jobs, with kids, with other obligations.

There really are a million excuses—good ones! A million valid reasons to just pick up a dozen cupcakes at the bakery for a child's party or a loaf of store-bought bread for a potluck and order the turkey-and-dressing package from the supermarket for Christmas dinner.

Don't get me wrong. There's absolutely nothing wrong with taking shortcuts. In fact, I think shortcuts can be crucial in making the Christmas Kitchen a real possibility in many people's lives. (You'll find a lot of them in this book!) Not everything needs to be made from scratch. Not everything needs to be done the way Grandma did it—or even the way you've been told is the "right way." And not everyone is in a position to throw a big party or even stage a traditional Christmas dinner.

But if you've picked up this book, I know something about you. I know you don't really want a prefab, carryout, catch-as-catch-can Christmas season. You certainly don't want a hectic, stressful, overworked holiday season where you wear yourself out meeting everyone's unrealistic expectations. Instead, you dream about a Christmas that is beautiful, special, warm, delicious, and as stress-free as possible. In some part of your heart, the Christmas Kitchen lives in all its intoxicating glory. And I'm here to tell you it can be part of your life—regardless of your circumstances, your kitchen skills, or your time limitations, and with far less stress and work than you ever expected.

The Christmas Kitchen, you see, isn't just a collection of appliances, recipes, and techniques. It's really a state of mind and heart, and the best way to get there is to adjust your thinking.

How?

A good place to start is to let go of perfection. Perfectionism can paralyze you, while an attitude of "good enough" can set you free.

Next, I encourage you to embrace the principle of true hospitality—not performing for others or impressing them or "entertaining" them, but using your life and your home (including your kitchen) to communicate to people how much you value them.* And it's not just something you do for guests but also for your family—and for yourself!

I hope you'll also promise yourself, no matter what, to enjoy the experience of Christmas, to laugh and celebrate and sometimes sit in silent wonder. It would be such a shame to be so caught up in activities, kitchen or otherwise, that you end up missing Christmas in your heart.

And finally, when you've wrapped your mind around a different approach to a beautiful Christmas, I urge you to start simply . . . but simply start. That's so important! Take just one step beyond dreaming and do just one delicious thing to make your Christmas season merry and bright.

It really doesn't have to be much. Maybe your one thing will be to just sit quietly, read this book, and dream while sipping a warm mug of holiday cider.

But that's the beauty of it—because once you do that one simple thing, I predict you'll find yourself wanting to do something else. And before you know it, your kitchen really will be Christmas Central, a true gathering place for making memories and serving up holiday joy for family and friends old and new.

Are you ready? I am. Let's take our first simple step into the Christmas Kitchen.

* Thanks to my dear friend Phyllis Stanley for teaching me about real hospitality. She'
the one who taught me that hospitality is "giving people a message about their valu

A Seasonal Sip—Blushing Mulled Cider

Start your season simply and warmly with a quiet moment and a mug of holiday cider. Wait till the kids are napping, turn off the phone, and take fifteen minutes to dream. The aroma alone will help put you in the holiday spirit.

1½ quarts apple cider

2 cups cranberry juice cocktail or cherry cider

¼ cup light brown sugar, or to taste

1 spice packet (page 12)

1 large orange, sliced

Simple Hints

You can make this delicious beverage in a slow cooker. Just combine the ingredients and simmer on HIGH for 3 hours. Remove spice packet and keep warm.

If you don't want to make up the spice packets, just put 1 teaspoon allspice berries, 1 teaspoon whole cloves, and 1 cinnamon stick in a tea ball or coffee filter. You can even use ground spices, in a pinch. Tie the filter into a bundle with kitchen twine or dental floss and add to cider.

Combine the cider, cranberry juice, and sugar in a saucepan. Add the spice packet. Cook and stir until the sugar is dissolved and cider is hot. Simmer gently for 30 minutes, then fish out the spice packet. Ladle into mugs and garnish with orange slices. Makes 6 servings.

Spice Packets for Cider and More

1 tablespoon allspice berries

1 tablespoon whole cloves

2 tablespoons crushed cinnamon sticks (place in plastic bag and crush with a rolling pin or edge of a plate)

1½ teaspoons dried chopped orange peel

1½ teaspoons dried chopped lemon peel

¾ teaspoon black peppercorns

Twelve 6-inch squares cheesecloth

Kitchen twine, food-safe ribbon, or unwaxed dental floss

• • • • • • • • • • • • • • • •

Mix the allspice, cloves, cinnamon, orange and lemon peels, and peppercorns together in a bowl. For each packet, use two cheesecloth squares and position kitty-corner on top of each other so that eight points are visible. Place one-sixth of the spice mixture (about 2½ teaspoons) in the middle of the doubled square and tie into a bundle with the twine, leaving one end of the twine longer for dipping. To give as a gift, place several spice bundles in a small tin and tie it with a bow and several sticks of cinnamon. Add a label with the following directions: "Place bundle in 2 quarts of cider or apple juice. Add ¼ cup light brown sugar, if desired. Heat at least 20 minutes." Makes 6 bundles,

These little bundles make wonderful gifts, but I also love to keep them ready for a delicious cup of cider at home.

Simple Hint

To make individual packets, use 4-inch squares of cheesecloth. Combine 2 or 3 allspice berries, 2 or 3 whole cloves, a ½-inch piece of stick cinnamon, a pinch each of dried orange and lemon peel, and 1 or 2 black peppercorns in each cheesecloth bundle. Pour cider in a microwave-safe mug, add a little cranberry juice if you want, and add the spice bundle. Microwave on HIGH 3 minutes, then let spices steep a few more minutes. Remove the bundle, sweeten to taste and enjoy.

Simple Hint

To dry orange or lemon peel, finely chop the peel, spread it on parchment paper laid on a cookie sheet, and bake in a warm oven (about 250ºF) until dry. Shake the cookie sheet occasionally to make sure the peel dries evenly.

Secrets to a (Relatively) Stress-Free Christmas Season

❋ Plan ahead. Your plans should include whys and whats as well as to-dos.

❋ Take shortcuts—lots of them! Save your effort for what you enjoy most.

❋ Accept the realities of where you are right now. Adapt your plans to your circumstances—but try to dream a little, too, and stretch yourself. Do what you comfortably can—and maybe one more little thing.

❋ Resist the urge to spend instead of give.

❋ Don't be driven by "the shoulds." Do only what matters most to you and your family—and make sure everybody has a voice.

❋ Celebrate tradition, but don't be ruled by it.

❋ Don't compare your Christmas to anyone else's—and try not to compare it to Christmases past.

❋ Try to make at least part of your Christmas a ministry, to those you love and to those God brings into your life.

❋ Think of ways to help your family enjoy a holiday from the ordinary. Let decorations, foods, and activities communicate the message that this is a special, unique time of year. Even if you're pinching pennies, find a few ways to splurge.

❋ Protect and nurture your sense of celebration. Take the time to let Christmas feed your spirit. Let Christmas come to you.

Chapter 2

Christmas Kitchen Prep

Preparing your home and your heart for a season of comfort and joy

When I was a little girl, I always thought Christmas would never come. These days it seems to barrel down on me like a fully loaded, beautifully decorated freight train.

So many possibilities! So much to do—so very, very soon! Seems like I barely have a chance to get aboard before the Christmas train goes roaring past.

It's not that I don't look forward to Christmas. I love Christmas. I even love the bustle (usually), the crowds (sometimes), the parties (almost always), and the excitement of putting it all together. But is it possible to have the magic without becoming stressed-out and exhausted?

I believe it's not only possible—it's crucial. What makes the difference is advance planning—a little Christmas Kitchen prep.

I don't mean churning out reams of lists and checking them twice (or more). I'm not talking about poring over a calendar to shoehorn in every possible activity. That's what many of us do. We just stack Christmas on top of our busy everyday lives. And that's what makes us tired!

Lists and calendars are helpful tools. I use them all the time. But they're not the place to start when it comes to getting ready for the Christmas season.

I love the Christmas hymn that urges, "Let every heart prepare Him room." Because that's where the most meaningful Christmases begin: with preparing our hearts and our lives (kitchens included!) for a season that is full of joy and, yes, peace.

So how do you prepare for the Christmas train that's already on its way? I believe you'll find your Christmas far more peaceful if you make the time well before the holidays to do these four things:

* ❄ *Take stock* of what you have, what you need, and—most important—what you want from this particular Christmas season.
* ❄ *Make room* in your life for the Christmas you want. This means clearing space in your calendar, your home, your heart, and your kitchen so you can enjoy special Christmas activities without clutter, stress, and overload.
* ❄ *Stock up* on items you're sure to use during the holidays. Take advantage of sales to gather baking supplies, freezer containers, gift wrap, batteries—whatever you think you'll need.
* ❄ *Make ahead*. Preparing meals and goodies in advance can help you be ready for hospitality at a moment's notice as well as feed your household on those hectic days when you can't even think, not to mention cook. (More on this in chapter 3.)

Once you've taken a little time to prep, you're ready to launch into the season. For me, as for many people, the Christmas season kicks off with Thanksgiving—and I love that! Celebrating God's gifts of harvest and of family segues naturally into celebrating the greatest gift of all: God's Son.

Our family loves to commence the Christmas season on Thanksgiving evening with the tradition of decorating gingerbread houses. That takes a little preparation on my part—but not as much as you might think, because I've gotten this activity down to a very fun science.

Remember what I said about taking shortcuts? I always take a big shortcut when it comes to our little gingerbread houses. I buy the pieces in ready-baked kits and glue them together with hot glue instead of icing. No one ever cares! After all, what people love about gingerbread houses is the decorating, and that goes just as well with the prefab, hot-glued gingerbread.

Just in case someone is pining for the spicy flavors, I do like to serve a delicious gingerbread on the side. But before I share that (fabulous) recipe with you, I want to add a word of encouragement for the times when you find yourself coming into Christmas unprepared.

It happens sometimes. It's happened to me. The Christmas train just roars on past with me running like crazy to catch up. But I'm learning that the joy and meaning of the season doesn't depend on planning or preparation or getting everything done. It doesn't depend on doing anything at all.

I mean it.

Christmas will still happen if you don't put up a tree.

It will still happen if you don't bake a single cookie or throw a single party, if you can't afford presents or don't have time to send out Christmas cards, or if all your plans go wrong.

It will even happen if you're sad or lonely or just not up to doing much. (I've had at least one Christmas like that.)

The reason we celebrate Christmas, after all, is that the Word became flesh and dwelled among us—and there were plenty of people who were less than perfectly prepared to receive Him. He came anyway. He changed the world. And that's still true, no matter what we do.

So when it's all said and done, the most important thing we can do to prepare for Christmas is simply to trust it. The gift of Christmas is there for you, and it comes without conditions. All you really have to do is open your heart and your hands to accept it. Everything else is (delicious) gravy.

A Holiday House-Raising

This is a beloved activity in our house. Every Thanksgiving evening, we gather to make these adorable gingerbread houses. Because I typically have a large crowd over for Thanksgiving, we like to divide into family teams (one family per house), but you could do this any way you want. If you're a small group, why not build a large house together? For each house you'll need the following:

✳ A ready-baked gingerbread house kit from a hobby or cooking store, or order online

✳ A base—I usually use a piece of heavy cardboard covered with foil

✳ Hot glue gun and glue sticks

✳ Icing cement to attach decorations (page 20)

✳ An assortment of candy, cookies, and other items for decoration (see Decoration Ideas for Gingerbread Houses, page 21)

✳ Friends and family to make the house!

Icing Cement for Gingerbread Houses

2 large egg whites

1/8 teaspoon cream of tartar

2 teaspoons water

3 cups sifted confectioners' sugar

• • • • • • • • • • • • • •

With an electric mixer, beat the egg whites, cream of tartar, and water until frothy. Beat in the sugar on high speed until stiff, 5 to 10 minutes. Use immediately or cover, refrigerate, and use within 8 hours. (Icing made with powdered egg whites doesn't need refrigeration.) Makes about 1½ cups

This kind of icing, also called royal icing, dries hard and is perfect for attaching decorations to gingerbread houses. Use this recipe or purchase a can of dried egg whites and follow the recipe on the label for royal icing. (If you plan to eat the icing, use the powdered egg whites.) Either way, plan to make extra batches. Keep the icing covered with a moist towel when not in use. And keep extra ingredients on hand to make more—we always run out!

Decoration Ideas for Gingerbread Houses

This is the fun part. Use your imagination and set out a variety of goodies to decorate the houses. The list below is just a start!

❄ *Candy*: gumdrops; chocolate bars and kisses; peppermint sticks, canes, and rounds; licorice; cinnamon candies; candy wafers; caramel squares and rolls, such as Tootsie Rolls; jelly beans; hard candies; breath mints; Gummi candies

❄ *Marshmallows*: white and colored; marshmallow snowmen, Santas

❄ *Chewing gum*: small squares; colored and striped strips

❄ *Fruit leather and candied fruits*

❄ *Cookies and crackers*: vanilla and chocolate wafers; graham crackers; cookie shapes

❄ *Cereal*: miniature shredded-wheat biscuits, plain and frosted; square checkerboard cereal, such as Chex; round oat cereal, such as Cheerios

❄ *Pretzels*

❄ *Ice cream cones*

❄ *Raisins; cranberries; nuts,* especially sliced almonds

❄ *Spices*: cinnamon sticks, allspice berries, whole cloves, whole nutmeg

❄ *Cake decorations*: gel icing in tubes; sprinkles; nonpareils; confectioners' sugar

Gingerbread on the Side

1½ cups light brown sugar

1 to 1½ cups granulated sugar, depending on taste

1 cup vegetable oil

4 large eggs

2/3 cup apple cider or water

One 15-ounce can pumpkin or 2 cups fresh pumpkin puree

3½ cups all-purpose flour

2 teaspoons baking soda

1½ teaspoons salt*

½ teaspoon baking powder

3 teaspoons ground ginger

1½ teaspoons ground allspice

1½ teaspoons ground cinnamon

1½ teaspoons ground cloves

½ teaspoon ground nutmeg

This is the best gingerbread—a variation on a recipe given to me by a dear friend in Dallas named Susan Lovvorn. It practically melts in your mouth, and it makes a wonderful gift. You can make it as muffins, mini loaves, or big loaves. But any way you bake it, it won't last long.

Simple Variation

Add golden raisins, dried cranberries, chopped pecans, chocolate chips, cinnamon chips or a combination. Amounts can vary—I use about 1 ½ to 2 cups total.

Simple, Healthier Variation

Replace the oil with unsweetened applesauce and sweeten with bake-able artificial sweetener such as Splenda. Still tastes great!

Preheat the oven to 325°F. Grease two 9 by 5-inch loaf pans, two 12-count muffin tins, or six miniature loaf pans (approximately 5 ¾ by 3 ¼ inches). In a medium bowl, beat the sugars, oil, and eggs until smooth. Add the cider and beat until well blended. Beat in the pumpkin. In a large bowl, mix together the flour, baking soda, salt, baking powder, ginger, allspice, cinnamon, cloves, and nutmeg. Add the pumpkin mixture and stir just until incorporated. Pour the batter into the pans and bake 70 minutes for large loaves, 25 minutes for muffins, or 45 minutes for mini loaves. The gingerbread is done when a toothpick inserted in the center comes out clean. Serve warm with whipped cream, top with Easy Cream Cheese Frosting (page 23), or simply sprinkle with a little confectioners' sugar. Makes about 24 servings, depending on portion size

*Unless otherwise indicated, all recipes in this book use regular iodized table salt.

Easy Cream Cheese Frosting

This recipe will frost 24 muffins, 2 loaves, or a 13 by 9 by 2-inch cake. Double the recipe to fill and frost an 8- or 9-inch layer cake.

One 8-ounce package cream cheese, softened

½ cup (1 stick) unsalted butter (no substitutes!), softened

2 to 3 teaspoons vanilla or almond extract

6 to 6¼ cups confectioners' sugar, sifted

1 teaspoon pumpkin pie spice (optional)

● ● ● ● ● ● ● ● ● ● ● ● ● ● ● ●

Beat the cream cheese, butter, and vanilla with an electric mixer until light and fluffy. Gradually add 1 cup of the sugar, beating well. Continue to beat in sugar to reach spreading consistency. Beat in the spice, if desired. Makes about 2 cups

Simple Variation

To make chocolate cream cheese frosting, prepare as above but beat ½ cup sifted unsweetened cocoa powder into cream cheese mixture and reduce the sugar to 5¼ to 6 cups.

Simple Hint

I freeze this frosting if I have extra. It keeps its texture and spreads beautifully when thawed.

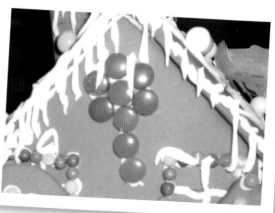

Stocking Up for Christmas

Look for these items at before-Christmas sales and year-round at white sales, discount stores, closeout shops, even yard sales.

❉ Wrapping paper and ribbon: buy it in bulk in just a few coordinating colors (metallics, red and green, blue and white, pink and orange—whatever fits with your taste and your decor)

❉ Glass or silver candlesticks in a variety of sizes

❉ Clear glass or white bowls, pitchers, flowerpots, candleholders, and hurricanes

❉ Candles: votives, pillars, tapers to match your decor and holiday mood

❉ Serving and baking dishes, including clear plastic disposables

❉ Special Christmas dishes: perhaps a new set of soup bowls or mugs to coordinate with your other dishes

❉ Gifts: for your family, friends, hosts/hostesses, and guests

❉ Silk flowers and greenery

❉ Pedestals: invaluable for adding dimension to a beautiful buffet table (see chapter 5)

❉ Small boxes, decorated boxes, and tins for packaging food gifts

❉ Permanent markers and paint pens

❄ Spices (allspice, cinnamon, both sticks and ground, cloves, ginger, nutmeg) and dried herbs such as sage, rosemary, and parsley. Even if you have these on hand, consider replacing them before the holidays if you've had them awhile.

❄ Baking ingredients (flour, sugar, confectioners' sugar, baking soda and powder, extracts) and tools such as cookie sheets

❄ Zippered plastic bags and freezer containers

Chapter 3
Make-Ahead Merrymaking

Cooking together for a joyful, stress-free holiday

Can the Christmas Kitchen be the Christmas Kitchen with just one person in it? Absolutely.

But I believe the Christmas Kitchen really comes to life in all its festive glory when many hands share the work—and the fun. There's just something about pitching in together that brings the holidays alive. Even better, cooking together makes preparing for the holidays a lot less stressful.

This is actually the way people used to prepare for holiday meal making and gift giving and entertaining. But things are different now, with many of us ensconced in our single-family dwellings, dishing up meals for our single families . . . or maybe just for ourselves. We're busy people and lonely cooks, and I believe that's one reason the holidays can feel like a burden.

But it doesn't have to be that way. Why not rediscover the fun of gathering in the Christmas Kitchen by scheduling a time to share the cooking or what you've cooked with friends, enjoying your time together while stocking your freezers with delicious food for the holidays?

One way to do this is to plan a food exchange—a gathering where participants bring and share precooked goodies but spend most of the time enjoying one another and the season. A traditional cookie exchange is one example of this kind of gathering. Everybody goes home with multiple dozens of different cookies for holiday gift giving, entertaining, and sneaking from the freezer.

An even better idea, to my mind, is to set aside several hours—or a whole day—for a cooking party. I've done this for years, during the holidays and at other times. Sometimes it's a group of old friends—we just dive in and have fun doing together what we would otherwise be doing all by ourselves. Sometimes it's a teaching session for young women who lack experience in the kitchen. Sometimes it's my own kids and their friends.

However they're configured, these cooking get-togethers are always a highlight of my holidays. And they keep on paying benefits through the season as we all take advantage of the wonderful, home-cooked meals and goodies we've made together and stored away.

What does one of these cooking days look like? We decide on the recipes in advance, bring all the ingredients and tools to one house, and start cooking. We save time by combining tasks and mixing everybody's ingredients into huge batches. We also listen to Christmas music, nibble on snacks . . . and talk! We laugh together, share stories, and build relationships while we're chopping and measuring and stirring. When we're through, we bring home container after container of goodies for the freezer and the fridge.

And yes, all this requires some organization. But the best part is, you can share the work of organization, too. That's the real point of it all—to share, to help one another, to enjoy one another and the season to the fullest. All the wonderful food is just a fabulous, stress-relieving bonus.

Simple Idea

Even if you can't manage a cooking day or a dessert exchange, you can still apply the principles of stocking up and sharing to your holiday season. Buy several rotisserie chickens or pumpkin pies on sale and freeze them for future meals. Or make a deal with a friend to cook double entrees for dinner one night and trade off the extras.

Simple Idea

If you don't manage anything else this season, make up a double batch of Gourmet Hot Cocoa Mix (page 60) and keep it in your pantry along with a box of high-quality commercial cookies. You'll always have something delicious and seasonal ready to serve and enjoy.

A Christmas Kitchen Cook-Ahead Gathering

Here are some helpful suggestions for organizing a cook-ahead gathering with a few friends or family members to prepare meals for hospitality or home. I must credit an amazing book for many of the ideas of cooking ahead in quantity. *Once-a-Month Cooking* by Mimi Wilson and Mary Beth Lagerborg was absolutely revolutionary in my life, and I heartily recommend it to you.*

❄ Match the number of cooks to the size of the kitchen. A large kitchen may be able to handle four or even five friends, a small kitchen only two. The friend with the largest kitchen should be the host or hostess.

❄ Expand prepping possibilities by bringing in folding tables, using an outside grill (even in winter), and sharing slow cookers, pressure cookers, food processors, and stockpots.

❄ If possible, hire a babysitter so you can concentrate on cooking and enjoy socializing without little ones underfoot. Consider it an investment in a peaceful holiday.

❄ Decide in advance what dishes will be cooked and in what quantities. It's important to circulate all the recipes among participants to check on family preferences, food allergies, and such. Make sure everybody has the recipes and agrees on what to bring.

❄ Depending on how well equipped the host kitchen is, guests may need to bring knives, cutting boards, pots, mixing bowls, and specialty equipment such as a food processor. This is another thing to agree on in advance.

❄ It helps to have some large bowls for mixing large quantities of ingredients. If none are available, a roasting pan or stockpot will do.

*Mimi Wilson and Mary Beth Lagerborg, *Once-a-Month Cooking: A Proven System for Spending Less Time in the Kitchen and Enjoying Delicious, Homemade Meals Everyday* (New York: St. Martin's Griffin, 2007).

❄ Every participant should bring the necessary ingredients to cook for his or her family, extra pots or pans or appliances (if appropriate), and containers for storing the resulting dishes. Put out permanent markers and labels to write the name of the dish, the date, and—very important!—reheating or cooking instructions. You can use the markers to write directly on freezer bags or tape the labels to reusable dishes. (Be sure to stick them down well so they don't fall off.)

❄ For maximum efficiency, go through all the recipes ahead of time and group similar tasks. For instance, if you'll need a total of 12 cups chopped onions for all the recipes, plan to chop them all at once.

❄ Set out snacks and drinks in a special area, and don't forget to take breaks to enjoy one another and taste what you're cooking. This is a party!

❄ Consider making an extra set of entrees or meals and giving it as a gift from the whole group to a single mom, new parents, your pastor's family, or a senior friend.

❄ Plenty of recipes throughout this book adapt beautifully to make-ahead merrymaking. In addition to the ones in this chapter, try Mama Mia's Meat Sauce (page 44; freeze flat in zippered bags), French Apple Cake (page 75; freeze without sauce), Coconut Angel Cupcakes (page 85; freeze unfrosted), Feliz Navidad Tortilla Soup (page 102; freeze flat in bags or in inexpensive reusable plastic containers), and My Mama's Chocolate Cake (page 118; freeze layers and thaw before decorating).

Simple Idea

Another great way to share the Christmas Kitchen is to recruit a group of friends to staff a Meals-on-Wheels kitchen or soup kitchen.

Meemaw's Turkey Enchiladas

6 cups shredded cooked turkey or chicken

One 10¾-ounce can condensed cream of chicken soup, undiluted

One 8-ounce carton sour cream (low-fat or nonfat works fine)

One 4-ounce can chopped green chiles, juice included

4 cups shredded Monterey Jack cheese

4 cups Mexican-blend shredded cheese

1 medium yellow onion, finely chopped

1 heaping tablespoon minced garlic

One 6-ounce can black olives, drained and sliced or one 14½-ounce can black beans, rinsed well (optional)

2 tablespoons ground cumin

1 bunch cilantro, chopped

1 quart chicken or turkey broth

Nonstick cooking spray

Ten to twelve 10-inch flour tortillas (try sun-dried tomato or pesto flavors for a green or red Christmasy look)

This is one of my favorite make-ahead recipes—and a fabulous way to use leftover Thanksgiving turkey or chicken. This recipe originally came from Beverly Wendt by way of her daughter, my friend Susan Kennedy, but I've changed it to suit my tastes. I like to use disposable foil pans for easy freezing, cleanup, and gift giving.

Simple Variations

Add a 4-ounce can of diced jalapeños (about ½ cup), drained, in addition to green chiles. Add an 8-ounce jar of marinated artichoke hearts, chopped, and ½ cup of dry-packed sun-dried tomatoes (no need to rehydrate). Roll several leaves of baby spinach into each enchilada. For vegetarian enchiladas, omit the poultry, substitute vegetable broth, and use 2 cans each of black beans and garbanzo beans, drained.

• •

To make the filling, combine the turkey or chicken, soup, sour cream, chiles, Monterey Jack cheese, 2 cups of the Mexican-blend cheese, onion, garlic, black olives (if using), cumin, cilantro, and ¼ cup of the broth to form a firm mixture. Spray a 13 by 9-inch pan with cooking spray. Fill each tortilla with approximately 2 heaping tablespoons of the chicken mixture, roll, and place seam down in the pan. Mix any remaining filling with the rest of the broth (it will be runny) and spread over the top of the enchiladas. Sprinkle the remaining Mexican-blend cheese over the top. Freeze at this point if desired, or bake uncovered in a preheated 350°F oven 25 to 30 minutes until bubbly.

To bake the frozen enchiladas, thaw overnight in the refrigerator and bake as above or bake the frozen casserole for about 1 ¼ hours, until bubbly. Makes 10 to 12 servings

Four-Way Cream Cheese Butter Cookies

The best thing about this wonderful cookie recipe (beside the great taste) is its versatility. One recipe makes four different kinds of cookies, all of which freeze well and are wonderful for a cookie exchange.

Simple Variations

Almond Spritz For colored cookies, add food coloring a drop at a time until desired color is reached. Place the dough in a cookie press and follow the manufacturer's directions to form shapes ½ inch apart on an ungreased cookie sheet. Decorate as desired with sprinkles. Bake 12 to 15 minutes, until cookies are golden brown on the peaks and bottoms. Remove from the cookie sheets at once and cool on wire racks.

Pecan Thumbprints Omit the almond extract and use 2 teaspoons vanilla. Chill the dough about 1 hour. Form into 1-inch balls and roll in finely chopped pecans. Place on an ungreased cookie sheet, ½ inch apart. Indent each cookie with your thumb and bake 12 to 15 minutes at 350°F. Cool as for spritz. When cool, fill the thumbprints with the jam of your choice.

Wedding Cookies Omit the almond extract and use 1 ½ teaspoons vanilla. Stir in ½ cup finely chopped pecans and ½ cup miniature chocolate chips. Chill the dough about 1 hour. Form into 1-inch balls. Place on an ungreased cookie sheet, ½ inch apart. Press down slightly on each ball. Bake 12 to 15 minutes at 350°F. Cool about 5 minutes, then roll in confectioners' sugar.

Cinnamon-Orange Wafers Substitute orange extract for the almond extract. Add 2 teaspoons orange zest or marmalade and ½ teaspoon ground cinnamon. Chill and form into 1-inch balls. Place on an ungreased cookie sheet, 1 inch apart. Use a sugar-dipped drinking glass to gently press into ¼-inch wafers. Bake 8 to 10 minutes at 350°F. (Because these are thinner, they may bake more quickly.) Cool on wire racks. If desired, when completely cool, glaze with a thin mixture of confectioners' sugar and orange juice.

1 cup (2 sticks) unsalted butter, softened

One 3-ounce package cream cheese, softened

1 cup granulated sugar

1 large egg yolk

1 teaspoon vanilla extract

1 teaspoon almond extract

2¼ cups all-purpose flour

¼ teaspoon salt

● ● ● ● ● ● ● ● ● ● ● ● ●

Preheat the oven to 350°F. In a medium bowl, cream together the butter and cream cheese. Add the sugar and egg yolk and beat until light and fluffy. Stir in the extracts. Sift the flour and salt in another bowl. Gradually blend into the cream cheese mixture. Finish as indicated below. Makes about 6 dozen cookies

How to Enjoy a Stress-Free Cookie Exchange

Here are some ideas I've gathered over the years for a cookie exchange that is simple and fun—a true joy instead of a chore.

❄ The perfect number of people for a cookie exchange is twelve, including the hostess. (This works well because most cookie recipes yield dozens.)

❄ Each participant bakes thirteen dozen of one kind of cookie: twelve dozen for sharing and a dozen for sampling.

❄ Check in with the hostess ahead of time to be sure recipes aren't duplicated, and make sure every cookie freezes well. In general, hard, crisp cookies freeze better than soft, chewy ones, and bar cookies (even soft ones) freeze best of all.

❄ For an efficient cookie exchange, each participant should bring twelve packages of a dozen cookies each, already packaged for the freezer. Each container should be labeled clearly with the type of cookie, the date they were made, and—important!—the recipe. The remaining dozen goes on a platter for sampling.

❄ Every participant should also bring a large carton to take home the cookies.

❄ At the party, the cookie exchange itself goes quickly. Each guest simply picks up twelve already-packed containers and puts them in his or her carton.

❋ Once the "business" part of the cookie exchange is over, it's time for the party. You already have the goodies: all those sample plates. All you need to add is something delicious to drink—coffee, hot tea, and perhaps some mulled cider.

❋ Put out pens and paper so guests can jot down notes about the cookies as they sample them.

❋ While you all munch, share a Christmas story or devotional, have a guest or two recall a memorable Christmas, or ask participants to share tips for making the holidays more meaningful.

❋ With your cookie exchange an unqualified success, consider a variation for next year. Try a theme—all chocolate cookies, all frosted cutouts, all bar cookies—or a cookie dough exchange, where each person brings twelve containers of prepared but unbaked goodies. Or why not try an entree exchange for a smaller group? Each person brings multiple recipes of a freezable entree already packaged and ready to go.

Chapter 4

Delicious Decor

Warm ideas for decking halls and hearts

Deck the halls, the carol invites us.

And so we do—with garlands and glitter, lights and ornaments and candles and beloved heirlooms we set out year after year. And not just the halls, but living rooms, family rooms, bedrooms, and dining rooms.

The kitchen, too?

Of course! I love to deck out my Christmas Kitchen for the season. But the kitchen has more to do with decorating than just draping a garland on a fridge, switching to seasonal kitchen towels, or even putting up a kitchen tree.

Decorating from the Christmas Kitchen involves creating objects that are beautiful to the eyes. Pomegranates and baby oranges tucked in among the greenery. Creamy candles bathing rooms in warm, flickering light. Sparkling crystal on a crisp white tablecloth.

Magic!

It involves spicing the home with enticing, evocative, familiar fragrances—nutmeg, apples, sage, vanilla, and orange—that hint at something wonderful simmering on the stove or baking in the oven.

Irresistible!

It means setting the stage for hospitality: spreading the table with snowy linen (or rustic red or gold brocade), using flowers and greens and silver and crystal to create a gentle or spectacular background for the special foods of the season.

And because decorating, like cooking, works well as a shared activity for family or gathered friends, decorating from the Christmas Kitchen may well involve feeding the decorators. A wonderful spaghetti supper tops off an evening of tree trimming as a star or heirloom angel tops the tree.

For me, decorating the house—including the kitchen—is all about anticipation. Beautifully decorated rooms set the stage for the real business of the season: people talking, laughing, singing, making connections, renewing friendships, healing wounds, building relationships, and sharing the wonder of what Christmas really means.

How you approach decorating will depend on a lot of things: your personal taste, your heritage, your pocketbook, where you live, and your stage of life. If you have small children, for instance, you'll want nontoxic, childproof decor. If you've been in your home a long time, you probably have many years' worth of collected decorations—the Nativity set, the Advent wreath, candles for the mantle, special pillows and afghans. I can relate. When I moved recently, I gave away box after box of decorations—and I still have plenty left.

I have learned a principle, however, that helps me decorate lavishly but without a cluttered look. That principle is: Whenever you add something, you must take away something else. When the Nativity scene comes out, the knickknacks from that table go into

the Nativity scene box and into storage. A tree goes up in my kitchen, my big decorative urns come down . . . and so on.

I find that if I stick to this principle, my house not only looks more beautiful, less cluttered, more festive, and wonderfully peaceful—it looks like a whole new house! The change in decoration reinforces the sense that something special is going on, creating the anticipation and ambience that help make Christmas feel like Christmas. And each year brings a fresh opportunity to do it again—to create a welcoming, warm, and fragrant atmosphere—courtesy of the Christmas Kitchen.

Decking Your Christmas Kitchen

❄ Invest (a small investment) in a Christmasy set of kitchen linens—potholders, towels, even a bright red pot scrubber.

❄ Put up a tree and decorate it with cookie cutouts (and cutters) and garlands of cranberries, popcorn, and dried citrus rounds (slice thin and bake in a 375°F oven until dried, then string on dental floss). Or buy a beautiful, fragrant rosemary tree and trim it with little ribbons.

❄ Find a place for a candle—or several. I always have candles in all my rooms, even the laundry room.

❄ Drape a greenery garland or twinkle lights (or both) above your cabinets.

❄ Create a simple but beautiful centerpiece for your kitchen table: a big glass or pottery bowl of crisp red apples or pinecones and cinnamon sticks.

❄ If your family observes Advent, the kitchen table is a lovely place for your Advent wreath.

❄ If it fits your taste and decor, hang a seasonal piñata from the ceiling.

❄ Frame an especially beautiful Christmas card or two and replace what's on the wall for the season.

❄ If you've collected Christmas dishes—mugs, bowls, platters—bring them out for display (and put your usual display items away).

Setting a Beautiful Christmas Table

❄ You don't need a lot of fancy dishes to set an elegant Christmas table. Start with a simple set of white or cream dishes and some serving bowls and platters in the same color. (They don't have to match exactly.) Add sparkle and color with accessories such as table linens, flowers, candles, and greenery.

❄ Look for one-of-a-kind serving dishes in closeout stores, antique stores, and yard sales. If you want to invest in special Christmas dishes, I suggest starting with a set of soup bowls or salad plates in a pattern that coordinates with your basics.

❄ One of the simplest and most dramatic ways to dress up your table is to use chargers under your plates. Look for these in discount stores in gold, silver, cranberry, black, or whatever color you choose.

❄ Ornaments from a discount store make adorable, colorful napkin rings. Simply put the hanging loop around the napkin and lay the ornament on top—a supremely easy splash of "ta-da!"

❄ Make generous use of natural materials to decorate. God did such a beautiful job of decorating the earth, and you can never go wrong with following His lead. Bring in pine boughs from your yard, or visit a Christmas tree lot and ask for their trimmed-off branches; then add pinecones, magnolia leaves, nuts, and fruits such as pomegranates and adorable orange kumquats. Tuck greenery around the edges of platters. Make generous use of herbs and spices as garnish. But be careful using holly or mistletoe around food—they're toxic if ingested.

❄ For a wonderful and fragrant natural touch, bind evergreens and herbs together in bundles with florist's wire. Cover the wire with a big bow and tie the bundles onto the backs of your dining chairs.

❄ For a stunning Christmas centerpiece, choose your favorite glass bowl—I use three of them in different sizes. Put in fresh cranberries, baby oranges, and holly greens. Add water and float candles on top. You can also use whole lemons and limes or nuts in the shell with the cranberries and greens.

❄ Decorate liberally with candles—columns, votives, and tapers. A generous collection of cream-colored candles set into crystal holders of varying heights and sizes and clustered on a mirror creates an absolutely stunning tablescape or centerpiece. Use scentless candles near the food when serving meals. Everywhere else, seasonally scented candles are a great way to make your whole house smell Christmasy.

❄ If you don't have an extra table for a buffet, a sturdy folding banquet table is a worthwhile investment. Drape a floor-length cloth over the top, and no one will be the wiser!

❄ Create a three-dimensional tablescape that looks good with or without platters of food. (I leave mine up the entire month.) Drape the table in a white tablecloth, then use cardboard boxes in three sizes to create a cluster of platforms with different heights. Drape another tablecloth over the boxes and arrange it so it "flows" around them. Drape a garland of real or artificial greens over and around the boxes and add candlesticks of various sizes to the arrangement. When guests come, place some serving dishes on the box platforms and some on the table (use ceramic or glass pedestals from the discount store, if you have them). After the party, take away the dishes, brush away the crumbs, and the tablescape becomes pure decoration.

Making Decorating Magic

For beautiful, snowy table settings, look for white 100 percent cotton tablecloths at closeout shops or in the restaurant section of a discount club. These can be bleached so they always look fresh without requiring kid-glove treatment. I store mine loosely folded and draped over sturdy hangers in a closet.

My all-time favorite decorating item is tulle, that fine netting often used for wedding veils. You can find it in a rainbow of colors at a fabric or discount store for less than a dollar a yard. I buy it by the bolt at Christmastime and use it to drape over tree branches, wrap presents, tie as decorative bows or napkin rings, or lay over white tablecloths as festive table runners.

Lighting is one of the most effective ways to decorate and create atmosphere. In rooms where no one will be reading or doing close work, keep the lighting gentle and warm and make liberal use of candles, twinkle lights, and lamps.

Soak evergreen boughs in a bathtub full of warm (not hot) water for several hours, then pat dry before using for decoration. They'll soak up the water and stay fresh much longer.

One of my favorite decorating tools is a metallic paint pen in gold, silver, or copper. Use it to paint simple freehand designs (stars, spirals, stripes, and dots) on tapers or column candles. White or cream-colored candles look beautiful with gold embellishments; red candles take on an extra-rich look with copper; and blue candles are spectacular with silver. (Sometimes the paint pen will scratch up little grains of wax, but these are easily brushed off after the paint dries.) You can also use the pens to write guests' names on clear glass ornaments, tie the ornaments with bows to match the pens, and place them in stemmed water glasses as placeholders.

Mama Mia's Meat Sauce

2 pounds bulk Italian sausage

1 pound lean ground beef

5 cups chopped yellow onion (about 5 large or 7 medium)

Three 12-ounce cans tomato paste

Five 28-ounce cans plain crushed tomatoes in puree

Five 28-ounce cans diced tomatoes in puree

1 large red bell pepper, stemmed, seeded, and chopped

1 ¼ quarts water

¼ cup minced garlic

10 bay leaves

½ cup sugar

2 tablespoons chopped fresh marjoram, or 2 teaspoons dried

3 to 4 tablespoons chopped fresh basil leaves, or 2 heaping tablespoons dried

3 to 4 tablespoons chopped fresh oregano leaves, or 2 large tablespoons dried

1 bunch parsley, preferably the flat-leaf Italian kind, chopped (leaves only)

2 tablespoons kosher salt

This rich and authentic-tasting sauce will feed a crowd of hungry decorators, with plenty left over to freeze for the future. Combine with Anne's Special Holiday Salad (page 45) and Easy Breadsticks (page 62), and you have a complete meal.

Simple Variations

Add three 14-ounce cans artichokes, drained and chopped, with other ingredients. For extra flavor, use marinated artichokes or add a small (about 3.5-ounce) jar of capers, drained. For a spicier, creamy variation (thanks to my friend Tom Davis), use hot Italian sausage and stir 1½ cups heavy cream into the sauce just before serving or storing.

To make in a slow cooker, halve the amounts of all ingredients. Brown the meat, then put all ingredients except the herbs in a large slow cooker. Cook on LOW for 8 to 10 hours or on HIGH for 4 to 5 hours, adding herbs during the last half-hour of cooking.

● ●

In a large pot, cook and stir the sausage and beef with the onion until meat is brown. Drain off the fat and add the remaining ingredients. Bring the sauce to a boil, then reduce the heat to low and partly cover. Simmer 2½ hours, stirring occasionally. Remove bay leaf. After sauce is cooled, you can freeze meal-sized portions (about 1 cup per person) in freezer bags. Make sure they lie flat while freezing—I put mine on a cookie sheet. Once frozen, they'll stack easily and save space. Makes about 36 cups

Anne's Special Holiday Salad

My friend Anne sent me the recipe for this festive-looking salad. The dressing is so simple, you won't believe how good it is!

● ●

Preheat the oven to 350°F. Spread the pecans on a cookie sheet and toast until fragrant, about 6 minutes. Whisk together the oil, honey, mustard, orange juice, vinegar, and pepper in small bowl. Wash and dry the greens and combine with the onion in a large salad bowl. Right before serving, add the fruit, pecans, and dressing and toss. Makes 12 servings

1 cup pecan halves

2 tablespoons extra virgin olive oil

4 teaspoons honey

1 tablespoon Dijon mustard

½ cup fresh orange juice

¼ cup balsamic vinegar

¼ teaspoon cracked black pepper

12 cups mixed greens (I like a mix of spinach and red-leaf lettuce)

½ cup slivered red onion

½ cup dried cherries, dried cranberries, or drained mandarin orange sections

Chapter 5

Kids in the Kitchen

The messy joy of creating with pint-size cooks

Want to know the secret for a truly joyful, wonder-filled Christmas Kitchen?

Make room for a kid—or kids—in it.

Christmas, after all, is largely about children. It started with the coming of a child. It's at its sweetest and most glorious when seen through a child's eyes, experienced with the heart of a child. And to me, at least, no Christmas Kitchen is complete unless children share in its magic.

Children reaching into cookie jars.

Children standing on stools, sifting flour and licking bowls and beaters.

Children setting the table for a family breakfast or making place cards for a dinner party, listening to family stories as they work.

It's all great holiday fun—for kids and adults alike.

Yes, I realize that kitchen work might go easier and faster with the kids in another room watching TV. In fact, if you have little ones at home, you probably long for just an hour or two during the holiday season when you have your Christmas Kitchen all to yourself.

Believe me, I understand. There was a time when I had four children under the age of five, all underfoot in the kitchen. So I would never counsel you to swear off babysitters at holiday time. I would never suggest that every moment in your Christmas Kitchen needs to be a "teachable moment" or that kids need to be part of everything that happens there. Yet the holidays are much richer if we intentionally welcome little ones to share in the Christmas Kitchen . . . because what children bring to the kitchen is often the heart of Christmas.

After all, Christmas is about anticipation, and who anticipates more fervently than a child? Christmas is about memories and tradition, and most children I know are passionate traditionalists. (Do something fun or meaningful with them, and they always want to do it again.) Christmas is about joy and wonder, and who can be more exuberant, more wide-eyed, than a little one?

Having kids in the kitchen can be a true Christmas gift, both for them and for us. We teach them, and we end up learning. We plan fun for them, and we end up enjoying ourselves. We make room for their inexperience and imperfection, and our own binding perfectionism relaxes. We introduce them to the wonder of Christmas, and we experience that wonder anew.

But none of this happens automatically. Just as we must prepare room for the Christ Child in our hearts each Christmas, so I believe we must prepare room in our hearts—and our kitchens—for little ones. As we make the Christmas Kitchen a safe and welcoming place for them, we welcome a little more of Christmas into our hearts.

So if you're a parent, I urge you to make your children a part of your Christmas Kitchen. If you're not a parent, or if your children are grown, why not borrow some pint-size cooks? Think of some harried parents you know and offer to take their kids off their hands for a Saturday afternoon . . . long enough to whip up a batch of cookies or do a simple craft or have a little party.

There are so many ways to include children in your Christmas Kitchen, and you can do it with much less stress than you might think. Make time, make space, and plan for things not to go exactly as planned. Above all, have fun, and enjoy anew the meaning of the season. Let the kids show you the way. You'll all be richer—and your Christmas Kitchen will be warmer—for the experience.

(Stress-Free) Fun with Kids in the Kitchen

❄ Allow extra time for making crafts and recipes. If you're not in a hurry, everything will be a lot more peaceful.

❄ Expect a mess—but expect the kids to help with cleanup, too.

❄ Provide kids with appropriate-height work spaces (or sturdy stools) and, if possible, tools that fit their hands.

❄ Match the projects to the kids' maturity level and plan activities that everyone can participate in without frustration.

❄ Especially with small children, don't provide too many options for craft or food projects. Keep it simple.

❄ Whenever possible, let kids do the project (or their part in it) themselves. Don't do it for them and just let them watch, and don't insist they do things only one way.

❄ Do the activity with the children. (You'd be surprised how fun it can be to string macaroni on a piece of yarn!)

❄ Don't have too many rules, but make the basics very clear: "Wash your hands." "Always have an adult present." Rules for using the stove or knives will depend on the age of the children.

❄ Expect the unexpected—and enjoy it.

Cinnamon "Gingerbread" Ornaments

This activity is a classic. The ornaments are adorable, long lasting, and unbelievably fragrant. The recipe will require several small cans of cinnamon, so check a discount or closeout store or buy it in bulk online.

1½ cups ground cinnamon (about 6 ½ ounces), plus more for dusting

1 cup applesauce

1/4 cup white school glue

Simple Variations

For an extra-cute garland, use medium cookie cutters to make cinnamon "gingerbread" men and women and cut holes in their hands. Decorate as desired, then string together with 8-inch strips of twine or ribbon.

Cut the cinnamon dough into four identical 4 or 5 inch squares. Cut another square about ½ inch larger. If desired, use tiny canapé cutters to cut out designs from the squares or scallop one edge of each of the four equal squares. When dry, hot-glue the four squares together at the edges with the larger square on the bottom to form an open cube. Place on a table open end up and slip a votive candle (in a glass holder) inside. These cinnamon candleholders are pretty and fragrant set among greenery, and they make great gifts for children to give.

In a large bowl, mix together the cinnamon, applesauce, and glue until it resembles cookie dough. (Add a bit more applesauce or cinnamon if necessary.) Remove the mixture from the bowl to a sheet of waxed paper and knead until smooth. Put it back in the bowl, cover with plastic wrap, and let set for at least 30 minutes. Remove the dough and knead it a few more strokes. Shape into a flattened disk and roll between sheets of waxed paper until it's 1/4 to 1/2 inch thick. Cut into desired shapes with cookie cutters and use the end of a drinking straw to punch holes for hanging. Gently transfer the shapes to a piece of clean waxed paper and leave them out to dry. Turn the ornaments several times a day so they will dry evenly and the edges won't curl. (Drying will take several days, and the ornaments will shrink a little during this process.) When the shapes are completely dry, decorate as desired with paint and glued-on decorations. (I like to use white texture paint in a squeeze bottle to resemble icing.) Thread a ribbon through the holes to hang decorations on the tree.

"Thank You for Helping Me Grow" Christmas Snack Mix

One 14-ounce bag red and green candy-covered chocolate pieces such as M&M's

One 14-ounce bag red and green candy-and-chocolate-covered peanuts such as peanut M&M's

One 11-ounce red and green candy-and-chocolate-covered almonds such as almond M&M's

3 cups corn cereal squares such as Chex

3 cups rice cereal squares such as Chex

3 cups oat cereal circles such as Cheerios

4 cups small pretzel twists

One 16-ounce jar dry-roasted peanuts

1 can (about 9 ounces) mixed nuts or cashews

One 6-ounce package dried cherries, cranberries, or blueberries

2 pounds almond bark or three 11- to 12-ounce bags white chocolate chips

I want to thank Jennifer Peters for originally giving me the recipe for this beautiful and delicious snack mix, although I changed it a bit. It's easy to make, and kids love the pouring and mixing. It's also beautifully Christmasy. My kids made it for their teachers and packaged it in adorable flowerpots. It was always a hit.

Simple Hint

To make the gift package for teachers, pour mix into flowerpots lined with plastic wrap and "plant" an artificial poinsettia or other flower in each pot. Add a pretty bow and a card from your child that says "Thank you for helping me grow." The child can write or dictate a personal note: "I like you because . . ." "My best memory is . . ."

Mix together the candies, cereals, pretzels, nuts, and fruit in large bowl or jumbo (2.5 gallon) zippered plastic bag. In large microwave-safe container, melt the almond bark on HIGH, stirring after every 30 seconds. Carefully pour over the dry mixture and mix together thoroughly. Spread the mixture on parchment or waxed paper to cool, breaking up large clumps. (The mix will be coated but not completely white.) Makes about 15 cups

Simple Variation

For an even richer taste, substitute one 11-ounce package butterscotch chips for part of the almond bark or white chocolate. Delicious!

Simple Idea

A great activity for kids is making garlands to string on the tree or to decorate their rooms. Anything with a hole in it (such as pasta or cereal) or anything that can be poked with a needle (such as popcorn or fresh cranberries) can become a festive garland. For a cute and easy garland, supply young kids with blunt needles strung with yarn or dental floss. Have them string together various round candies with holes in them and colored drinking straws cut into 1- to 3-inch lengths. Older children will get a kick out of using a sharper needle and heavy-duty thread or dental floss to make garlands of cranberries and popcorn.

Reindeer Cupcakes

24 chocolate cupcakes topped with chocolate frosting

Chocolate sprinkles

24 small red gumdrops

48 small white oval mints such as TicTacs

48 pecan halves

48 pretzel twists

• • • • • • • • • • • • • •

Roll the tops of the frosted cupcakes in chocolate sprinkles. Create a "Rudolph the Red-Nosed Reindeer" face on each cupcake by using a gumdrop for the nose, mints for eyes, pecan halves for the ears, and pretzels for the antlers. (Break pretzels in half to make curved and branching antlers.) Or use your imagination with other candies, nuts, and food items (see the list on **page 21**) to make different kinds of designs. Makes 24 cupcakes

These are fun to make with children—great for parties at school or church or to give as a gift for your neighbors.

Simple Hint

It's fine to use a cake mix and purchased frosting, or you can even buy frosted cupcakes from a bakery.

Simple Ideas

One of my children's favorite activities when they were small was our annual birthday party for Jesus. The kids would help me bake a birthday cake, and they'd invite friends and neighbors. We would enjoy a simple Christmas craft or play a game, then bring out the cake and light the candles. The kids loved singing "Happy Birthday" at the top of their lungs . . . followed by carols and snacks.

Keep a small "kidproof" wooden Nativity scene in your kitchen for little ones to play with while you cook. It's a wonderful way to keep them occupied while introducing the true meaning of Christmas.

For a fun and giving afternoon with kids, decorate a "feed the birds" tree. This is a custom dating back to the sixteenth century, when people honored the birds and beasts that came to the manger. Choose either an outdoor evergreen or an old artificial tree set up for the purpose. (After Christmas, you can recycle your indoor trees for this purpose, but be sure they're free of ornaments, especially tinsel.) Decorate with items the birds will enjoy eating. Thread blunt needles with twine and let the children string chains of cranberries, raisins, cereal, and popcorn. Dip pinecones, pretzels, or shapes cut from stale bread into peanut butter, then roll in birdseed. Hang little apples and other fruits by their stems or hollow out oranges to make cups to fill with seed or crumbs. You can also add strips of thin ribbon, yarn, or fabric for the birds to use in building their nests. Make sure the tree is in a spot where you can watch from the window—one year we even put one up on our deck!

Chapter 6

From Our Home to Yours

Inspired gifts from your kitchen and from your heart

Christmas isn't (or shouldn't be) just about presents. Yet Christmas is (or should be) a festive celebration of giving—and the Christmas Kitchen is one of your best resources. It can be both an inspiration and a workshop for creating gifts that delight the heart and the soul . . . not to mention the taste buds. And giving from your kitchen is its own reward. What can be more satisfying than to whip up something beautiful and delicious, wrap it beautifully and imaginatively, and place it in someone else's eager hands?

The possibilities of what and how to give are limited only by your imagination. Gifts *from* the kitchen are a time-honored treat. There's just something about food that touches the heart, and you don't have to worry about sizes, colors, or decor. Gifts *for* the kitchen— refrigerator magnets, kitchen towels, serving platters, ingredients, even recipes—are another fresh alternative for giving.

A Christmas Kitchen gift can be small and simple, little more than a big cookie tied with a bow or a discount-store mug filled with candy. It can be beautiful and extravagant—a huge basket packed full of home-cooked delicacies or even an entire meal. It can be one of a kind, personally matched to the recipient, or stirred up in quantity and packaged assembly-line style—think dozens of cute little jars filled with goodies and tied with bows, ready to distribute to a list of friends.

And yes, if you let it, Christmas Kitchen gifting can become a chore, another "to-do" in a list of obligations. So it's not a bad idea to keep watch on your heart when you're making plans and recipes in your Christmas Kitchen. Examine your budget, your time, and your motivation . . . and try not to fall into the trap of thinking you need to give a material gift to every person every year. Sometimes a card will suffice. Sometimes a simple and heart-felt "Merry Christmas" is all you need.

But if your heart is telling you to think big this year, to dedicate a day or days to making gifts from the kitchen, I think you should listen. Much joy can be found in being a little extravagant, a bit over the top—putting a little more time and talent and money into your gifting than you can easily afford. It's Christmas, after all! So put on some holiday music, maybe invite someone to help you, and go for it. You can even make extras of whatever you're giving and keep them on hand for spur-of-the-moment gifting opportunities.

For maximum joy and satisfaction, give to at least one person who isn't expecting a gift—or who cannot give back. Adopt a needy family and bring them Christmas dinner. Prepare a lovely basket for a newly widowed person or a big basket of cookies for a family torn in two by divorce. Help stock and staff a food pantry . . . or load up the kids to help serve at a soup kitchen . . . or donate goodies to a bake sale to benefit a local charity.

Through it all, remember that the best gifts, after all, are simply messengers. They're concrete ways of saying "I see you," "I'm thinking about you," "I care about you," "I want to share this wonderful season with you." And there are many ways to send that message. A shared cup of coffee and a cookie can be a gift. A phone call or a note can be a treasured gift. A meal for your family is a gift of love. There's a gift in the stories that are told by the sink and stove, the memories that are made around the table.

All gifts from the Christmas Kitchen.

All fitting tributes to the One who is the greatest gift of all.

Gourmet Hot Cocoa Mix

4 cups instant nonfat dry milk powder

2 cups sifted confectioners' sugar

2 cups French vanilla powdered nondairy coffee creamer

2 cups powdered chocolate milk mix (the store brand works just fine)

One 5-ounce (6 serving) package cook-and-serve (not instant) chocolate pudding mix

¼ cup unsweetened cocoa powder

2 cups miniature marshmallows and/or miniature chocolate chips (optional, but yummy)

Boiling water or milk, for serving

● ● ● ● ● ● ● ● ● ● ● ● ● ● ●

Combine all the ingredients in a bowl and stir well. For a better blend, mix the dry ingredients in a blender or food processor before adding the marshmallows. Store the mix in an airtight container. Makes about 12 ½ cups mix, for 50 servings

To serve, place ¼ cup mix (or more) in mug or cup. Add ¾ cup boiling water or hot milk and stir well.

This fancy version of a traditional hot cocoa mix is a perfect and yummy gift for teachers and neighbors—but keep some at home, too, for your family and for impromptu hospitality. I love to add a little to my coffee.

Simple Variations

Minted Hot Cocoa Mix Omit the marshmallows and add 1 cup mint chocolate morsels.

Mexican Hot Cocoa Mix Omit the marshmallows and add 2 teaspoons ground cinnamon. If you're brave, stir in a little cayenne pepper, too.

Rich Mocha Mix Use mocha-flavored creamer and add 1 cup instant coffee granules to mix.

Guiltless Indulgence Combine 3 cups nonfat dry milk, 1 cup artificial sweetener (such as Splenda), ½ cup unsweetened cocoa powder, and one 1-ounce (4 serving) package fat-free, sugar-free vanilla pudding mix.

Simple Hint

To give as a gift, put the mix in a pretty covered glass container. Use ribbon to tie on two decorative mugs. (Deliver carefully to keep them from clanging around and breaking.) You could also attach miniature bottles of syrup such as cherry, amaretto, or Irish cream from a coffee shop; peppermint or cinnamon sticks for stirring; or a lovely ornament . . . use your imagination. Be sure to attach the recipe and instructions for use!

Simple Ideas

Always include recipes with any gift from your Christmas Kitchen. That way the recipients won't be calling up at inconvenient times to ask for it, they'll be forewarned of any ingredients they may be allergic to, and the recipe itself will be a bonus gift.

I always bring food (especially chocolate!) instead of flowers as a hostess gift. Wrapping it beautifully will give the message that you don't expect her to serve it immediately to the guests.

Easy Breadsticks or Pretzels

One 10 or 11-ounce package refrigerated pizza dough

Melted butter or extra virgin olive oil

Kosher salt or garlic salt

• • • • • • • • • • • • • • •

Preheat oven to 400°F. Unroll the dough on lightly floured work surface and shape into a 16 by 10-inch rectangle. Brush with the butter and sprinkle with salt. Cut into twenty-four 10-inch-long strips. If you wish, twist the strips into pretzel shapes. Place the strips or pretzels ½ inch apart on well-greased cookie sheets and bake for 10 minutes, or until golden brown. To reheat, bake at 350°F for 5 minutes. Makes 24 breadsticks or pretzels

A different-but-delicious gift, and so easy! Pack these breadsticks in a gift basket with two varieties of mustard or for an Italian basket, a container of Mama Mia's Meat Sauce (page 44) and a wedge of good Parmesan cheese, all in a basket lined with a checkered tablecloth.

Simple Variations

❄ *Spiced-Nut Pretzels* Place 1 cup finely chopped pecans and 1 tablespoon extra virgin olive oil in a plastic bag. Combine ½ teaspoon chili powder, ¼ teaspoon ground cumin, ¼ teaspoon ground cinnamon, and a dash of ground red pepper in a small bowl. Add the spice mixture to the nuts, seal the bag, and toss to mix thoroughly. Place the spiced nuts in a small skillet over medium heat and stir constantly until the nuts are lightly toasted. Sprinkle the nut mixture with 1 teaspoon garlic salt and cool to room temperature. Roll out the dough as directed above and sprinkle the nuts over the dough, pressing lightly to adhere nuts to dough, before cutting into strips and twisting into pretzels.

❄ *Ranch-Style Pretzels* Combine 2 tablespoons dry ranch-flavored dip mix with 2 tablespoons sour cream. Roll out the dough as directed on page 62 and spread the mixture evenly over the dough before cutting into strips and twisting into pretzels.

❄ *Parmesan–Puff Pastry Sticks* Use frozen puff pastry instead of pizza dough. Thaw the dough and place one piece on a piece of waxed paper that has been sprinkled with grated Parmesan, garlic powder, and Italian seasoning. Sprinkle more cheese and seasonings on top of dough and gently flatten with a rolling pin to work cheese into both sides of dough. Cut into strips with a pizza cutter, twist gently, and place on parchment-paper-lined baking sheet. Bake at 375°F for about 10 minutes. Let cool. Handle these breadsticks gently to keep from breaking.

Cracked Peppercorn Mustard

2½ cups prepared honey mustard

1 cup extra-grainy Dijon mustard

2 tablespoons freshly cracked black pepper

3 tablespoons chopped fresh tarragon leaves or 1 tablespoon dried

This mustard is yummy with homemade breadsticks and pretzels. It also makes a wonderful topping for grilled chicken.

• • • • • • • • • • • •

Combine all the ingredients in a bowl and blend with a wire whisk. Spoon into four labeled 1-cup glass jars. (These don't need to be sterilized but should be clean.) Cap tightly and label. Can be stored in the refrigerator for 4 weeks. Makes about 3 ¾ cups

Spicy and Sweet Mustard

2 cups spicy brown mustard

1 cup chunky peanut butter

¾ cup hoisin sauce

¾ cup packed light-brown sugar

1 teaspoon grated fresh ginger

Add Asian flair with this special topping.

• • • • • • • • • • • •

Combine all the ingredients in a bowl and blend with a wire whisk. Spoon into four clean 10-ounce glass jars. Cap tightly and label. Can be stored in the refrigerator for 4 weeks. Makes about 4 ½ cups

Pick a Basket

Here are some ideas for wonderful gift baskets you can put together from—or for—the kitchen. You don't have to use actual baskets, either. Corral your gifts in pretty bowls, candy dishes, bags, recycled boxes . . . use your imagination!

❄ *Snack Basket*: three flavors of snack mix—for instance, Teddy Bear Caramel Corn (page 92), Christmas Snack Mix (page 52), and Spicy Nut Mix (page 90)

❄ *Warm 'Em Up Basket*: Gourmet Hot Cocoa Mix (page 60), a decorative mug, and a scarf, hat, and mittens

❄ *Movie-Night Basket*: Teddy Bear Caramel Corn (page 92) or microwave popcorn packages, cookies, and a classic Christmas DVD

❄ *Firelight Basket*: homemade goodies, waxed pinecones for the fireplace, and long fireplace matches

❄ *Kitchen Basket*: homemade goodies, kitchen towels, refrigerator magnets, and a decorative potholder or oven mitt

❄ *Fiesta Basket*: gourmet chips, jar of salsa, container of spicy bean or cheese dip (store-bought or homemade), and Mexican Hot Cocoa Mix (page 60)

❄ *Mix It Up Basket*: stainless-steel measuring spoons, beautiful rolling pin, recipe cards, and spices

❄ *Bread Basket*: bread flour, yeast, bread tile or stone, a great recipe, and a loaf of the baked bread

❄ *Serve It Basket*: large serving platter stacked with Christmas linens and wooden spoons

❄ *Salt and Pepper Basket*: small food mill, mixed peppercorns, sea salt, and commerical herb mix (or just combine a variety of those little mills from the spice section of the grocery store)

❄ *Spice Basket*: small spice mill with jars of whole nutmeg, allspice berries, and whole cloves

❄ *Basket o' Chocolate*: Gourmet Hot Cocoa Mix (page 60), truffles, and some high-end candy bars

❄ *Salad Basket*: wooden salad bowl, serving tongs, jar of delicious gourmet or homemade salad dressing, and a plastic bag of homemade croutons

❄ *Instant Picnic*: picnic basket with cute, unbreakable dishes, cutlery, napkins, and a treat from your kitchen

❄ *Cup o' Tea Basket*: mugs or teacups with a canister of good loose tea or tea bags, sugar cubes, tea accessories such as small tea ball, sugar tongs, or strainer, and a bag of homemade cookies or biscotti

❄ *Java Basket*: decorative mugs, a pound of quality coffee, hand grinder, small bottle of flavored syrup or flavored nondairy creamer, and a bag of homemade cookies or biscotti

❄ *Mama Mia Basket*: jar of Mama Mia's Meat Sauce (page 44) or good commercial spaghetti sauce, package of whole-wheat spaghetti, wedge of excellent Parmesan cheese, and Italian bread or Easy Breadsticks (page 62)

❈ *Fruit and Cheese Basket*: several large apples or pears, wedge of smoked gouda or aged cheddar, cheese knife, and a bag of gourmet crackers or loaf of bread

❈ *Best Friend Basket (for a dog-loving friend)*: dog toy, gourmet (or homemade) dog biscuits, and a new collar or dog blanket

❈ *Literary-Moment Basket*: treasured book, bag of goodies, and a coffee cup

❈ *Dinner-in-a-Basket*: fully cooked entrée, salad, bread, and dessert (I give this gift every year to my pastor and his family, along with five or six additional meals that have been frozen. It's the gift that keeps on giving.)

Chapter 7

The Gift of Yourself

Intimate gatherings for your special friends

What are you giving your close friends this Christmas?

I'm talking about the friends you trust with your secrets, who help you, listen to you, are there when you need them. The great old friends you still love to spend time with . . . or the ones you've just gotten to know and would love to know better. What special gift can you give them this season that tells them exactly how much you value them?

You could spend many hours—and a lot of money—shopping for just the right item for each friend and wrapping it with care. You could set aside a special time to present each gift, a carefully chosen moment for the two of you.

And that would be wonderful.

But if you're like me, your holidays are usually so crammed that it's not going to happen. You're busy. Your friends are busy. Funds are tight and time is even tighter. And despite your best intentions, despite your love for each other, there simply aren't enough hours to do justice to each special relationship. So you make do with quick hugs or a phone call, plus a heartfelt promise to get together after the holidays.

And that's all right. Good friends understand.

But here's another possibility: Why not invite all your special friends to a lovely, intimate Christmas gathering, and make this time together your gift to them? For years that's been one of my favorite things to do during the holidays.

Usually ours is a daytime gathering—a sumptuous morning brunch, a delectable afternoon tea, a light lunch, even a simple coffee klatch. Many of my friends work outside the home, so I try to schedule our get-together for a Saturday or Sunday. I do everything I can to make it a warm, relaxed, affirming, and delicious time, an oasis of loveliness in the midst of all the Christmas chaos.

And my friends love it! They enjoy getting together, and they're supremely grateful when someone initiates such a gathering. It's a treat for them to be fed and pampered in beautiful surroundings, to have plenty of time to talk and do things together. And they positively glow when they are intentionally affirmed and encouraged. So those are the elements I always try to include in these special get-togethers.

As far as the details go, they vary from year to year. Some years it may be just five or six of my closest friends. More often, though, I'll invite ten to twenty women—a mix of old friends and new. It's a great way to introduce the people I've loved for twenty-plus years to those I've just recently come to appreciate. And I always make a special point to include my single friends, especially single moms, because I've learned that single women are often left out of group events.

I take special care with decorations and mood, making sure the candles are lit and the music is playing and the atmosphere is cozy and beautiful and inviting. I try to provide name tags, to make sure everyone knows each other. And I always greet each woman at the door with a big hug. Then we dig into something delicious and sip something warm and spicy. We talk, catching up on each other's lives or getting to know each other better and sharing funny and poignant stories of what life has handed us that year. Sometimes we'll sing carols, or we might do a little project together. (One year we decorated evergreen wreaths.) But whatever else we do, I always take time to go around the circle and intentionally affirm each woman, telling the whole group what she means to me, what I appreciate about her, why I'm grateful to have her in my life.

You should see my friends' faces when I do that—even when they've been to one of my gatherings before. No material gift could be more personal, more appreciated. Every woman I know longs to be told—from the heart—that she is loved.

And then, after a few delicious hours together, it's time to go. As each friend leaves, I'll give her another hug and a little gift—perhaps an ornament, a small potted herb, or a Christmas CD. Then we return to our hectic holiday lives.

But if I've done what I set out to do, each heart has been warmed, each life has been touched. I've truly given the gift of myself, and I've given myself the gift of my friends' company. For the rest of the day, I can't help smiling.

Try it. You'll smile, too!

Blueberries for Brunch

For the French toast

12 slices day-old bread, crusts removed

Two 8-ounce packages cream cheese (the
low-fat variety works fine)

Ground cinnamon

1 cup frozen or fresh blueberries

1 pound sausage, cooked and crumbled (I use
spicy Jimmy Dean's) or 1 cup chopped pecans

12 large eggs

2 cups milk

½ cup pure maple syrup

2 teaspoons vanilla extract

For the sauce

½ cup granulated sugar

½ cup packed light-brown sugar

1 tablespoon cornstarch

1 cup water

1 teaspoon ground nutmeg

2 cups fresh or frozen blueberries or other berry
(I like to use the frozen triple-berry mix from
the grocery store—blueberries, strawberries, and raspberries)

1 tablespoon unsalted butter

*This cross between French toast and bread pudding is per-
fect for brunch or for Christmas-morning breakfast. It's
especially suited to easy entertaining because you can make
it the day before. For a festive brunch, I like to serve it with
nonalcoholic mimosa coolers (see below) and good coffee.*

Simple Idea

Mimosa coolers make a refreshing beverage to go with brunch.
Simply mix orange juice and ginger ale. Pour over ice and
garnish with orange slices and maraschino cherries. Delicious!

Cut the bread into 1-inch cubes and place half in a greased 13 by 9-inch baking dish. Cut the
cream cheese into 1-inch cubes and place over bread. Sprinkle liberally with cinnamon. Top with
the blueberries and sausage, then remaining bread. Beat the eggs in a large bowl. Add the milk,
maple syrup, and vanilla and pour over the bread mixture. Sprinkle with more cinnamon. Refrigerate until ready to bake, up to a day or two ahead.

Remove from the refrigerator about 1½ hours before you plan to serve. Let sit for 30 minutes
while you preheat oven to 350°F. Cover with foil and bake 30 minutes, then uncover and bake
30 minutes more or until golden brown and the center is set. Makes 8 servings

To make the sauce, combine the sugars and cornstarch in a saucepan. Stir in the water and nutmeg
and bring to a boil over medium heat. Boil for 3 minutes, stirring constantly. Add the berries, reduce
the heat, and simmer 10 minutes. Stir in the butter until melted. Serve over the baked pudding.

Salmon and Lemon-Caper Cream Sandwiches

If your gathering takes the form of an afternoon tea, finger sandwiches are classic fare—and this filling is to die for.

½ cup mayonnaise

1 tablespoon drained capers

½ teaspoon finely shredded lemon peel

½ teaspoon Dijon mustard

1/8 teaspoon ground white pepper

32 slices bread (your choice—see Simple Hints, page 74)

Softened unsalted butter or mayonnaise

Curly endive or lettuce leaves

8 ounces thinly sliced smoked salmon or smoked turkey

Fresh dill, for garnish (optional)

• • • • • • • • • • • • • • • • • •

In a small mixing bowl, stir together the mayonnaise, capers, lemon peel, mustard, and pepper. Spread all the bread slices with butter or plain mayonnaise. Top half of the bread slices with greens. Divide the salmon or turkey over the greens. Top with 1 teaspoon of the mayonnaise mixture per sandwich and finish with the remaining bread slices. If desired, garnish with fresh dill. Serve at once. Makes about 16 servings

Curried Chicken–Cashew Sandwiches

½ cup plain yogurt

2 tablespoons soft-style cream cheese (from a tub)

2 tablespoons snipped chives or thinly sliced green onion (scallion), plus extra for topping

1 teaspoon curry powder

¼ teaspoon salt

1½ cups finely chopped cooked chicken or turkey (about 1 large chicken breast)

¼ cup finely chopped cashews or almonds

24 slices bread (your choice—see Simple Hints, on the right)

Softened unsalted butter or mayonnaise

Curly endive or lettuce

● ● ● ● ● ● ● ● ● ● ● ● ● ● ●

In a bowl, stir together the yogurt, cream cheese, chives, curry powder, and salt. Add the chicken and cashews and blend thoroughly. Spread the bread slices with the butter. Top 12 slices with greens and 2 tablespoons of chicken mixture. Top with additional chives or green onion and cover with the remaining bread slices. Makes about 12 servings

Here's another amazing tea sandwich that's great for luncheon as well.

Simple Hints

Use the bread of your choice to make tea sandwiches: regular white or wheat, pumpernickel or rye party slices, tiny croissants, or miniature bagels. (Using different breads may yield a different number of sandwiches.) If your bread has crusts, cut them off before filling. (You can stack six slices of bread at a time to cut off crusts quickly.) Always spread the bread thinly with butter or mayonnaise to keep it from becoming soggy.

The best tea sandwiches are practically bite-size. Use a serrated knife to cut large sandwiches into triangles or small squares. Or try cutting out simple shapes with a Christmas cookie cutter. If you do this after the sandwiches are filled, the cutter will seal the edges and help keep the filling from leaking out.

Hold sandwiches together with toothpicks stuck through a sprig of herbs or a slice of green stuffed olive, or sprinkle top of sandwich with chopped basil or dill. Arrange on a pretty platter topped with a paper doily.

For a very simple, delicious, and beautiful tea sandwich, spread thin slices of your favorite fruit-nut bread with flavored cream cheese spread from a bagel shop.

French Apple Cake with Caramel Sauce

This recipe was given to me by my sister Terri Sue. I added more spices to make it my own—I like it with a bit more kick. The recipe was a hit from the first time I brought it to a women's Bible study. The women were actually drinking the sauce! I always make a double recipe for that very purpose.

Simple Hint

The caramel topping is also delicious poured over baked apples.

Simple Hint

My amazing friend and mentor Phyllis Stanley always doubles the eggs in her Christmas baking—she claims this makes everything much richer. I feel the same about doubling the vanilla.

● ●

To make the cake, preheat the oven to 350°F. Generously grease a 13 by 9-inch baking pan. In a medium bowl, whisk together the sugar and eggs until frothy. Mix in the oil and vanilla. In a large bowl, mix together the flour, baking soda, salt, and spices. Add the egg mixture, nuts (if using), and apples. Pour the batter into the pan—it will be thick. Bake for 45 to 50 minutes or just until top springs back when lightly touched. Do not overbake. Allow to cool slightly.

To make the caramel sauce, combine all the ingredients in a heavy saucepan and bring to a boil. Boil about thirty seconds, stirring, or until thickened. Remove from heat.

To serve, cut the cake into squares, pour warm caramel sauce over each square, and top each with whipped cream or ice cream. Makes 12 servings

For the cake

2 cups sugar

2 large eggs

½ cup canola oil

2 teaspoons vanilla extract

2 cups all-purpose flour

2 teaspoons baking soda

1 teaspoon salt

½ teaspoon ground cloves

2 teaspoons ground cinnamon

½ teaspoon ground allspice

½ cup chopped walnuts (optional)

4 cups peeled and diced apples (I like Granny Smith or Jonathan)

For the caramel sauce

1 cup packed light-brown sugar

1 cup granulated sugar

1 cup heavy cream

½ cup (1 stick) unsalted butter

2 tablespoons all-purpose flour

3 teaspoons vanilla exract

Freshly whipped cream or high-quality vanilla ice cream

Chapter 8

Hope You Can Come!

Hospitality for your busiest season

If you're ever going to throw a party, Christmas is the time to do it.

The house is already decorated. The Christmas CDs are already in the player. You've got some goodies in the freezer or at least some great new recipes (read on!). So all you really need is a space on your calendar, some people to invite (they're everywhere around you), and a willingness to open your heart and your home for some fun and festivities.

Your Christmas Kitchen can cater any kind of celebration, from spur-of-the-moment cocoa and cookies to a full course meal. But to me, the easiest and most appreciated kind of party is a holiday open house featuring an array of hors d'oeuvres and finger foods. Such a party can be dressed up into something elegant or simplified into something casual and easygoing. It can accommodate any number of guests, all at one time or coming and going. It can take place almost any time of day and even share an evening with another activity or celebration—a concert, a play, or another party.

Best of all, most of the dishes can be prepared well ahead of time, freeing you to enjoy your guests—which, to me, is the heart of any event. Why even have a party if you're going to be sequestered in the kitchen the whole time?

You don't have to do all the work yourself, either. I often share hosting duties with a friend ("You help with my party; I'll help with yours!") and enlist my spouse and kids to help. Sometimes I'll hire a couple of my teenagers' friends to work the kitchen—whatever makes the workload lighter and the evening more fun.

And yes, I said fun. Fun needs to be a priority for you as well as your guests—and hosting a party really can be a blast!

So why not take the party plunge? Decide how many guests you can handle and whom you'd like to spend time with—and try to include someone new, someone lonely, someone outside your usual circle. Send invitations, make a few phone calls, or post an announcement on the office bulletin board. Have fun arranging your gorgeously decorated buffet table and filling your fridge with some fabulous, deceptively easy appetizers (again, read on). Hang a welcoming wreath or some jingle bells—or both!—on the door. Then put on your party clothes, sneak a delicious bite from the back of the antipasto platter, light the candles . . . and prepare to enjoy yourself.

Whatever else you do, try to meet each guest at the door. Offer him or her something wonderful to drink and, if it's a new crowd of people, a name tag. Make sure whoever rings your doorbell gets the clear message: "I'm really glad you're here. For the next few hours, your happiness and comfort is my goal." That, after all, is the whole point of any form of hospitality, including your festive Christmas party.

Hospitality, remember, is not about impressing people. It's not about competing to throw the best party of the season. It's not about swapping obligations or stressing yourself out to pull off a perfect event. Instead, it's about comfort and care. It's about reaching out to others, welcoming them into your life, using your home and your generous heart to make connections, build relationships, and share the celebration of the season.

And that, in itself, is reason enough to party!

Crabmeat Cucumber Rounds

1/4 cup mayonnaise

1 teaspoon prepared horseradish

1/2 teaspoon Dijon mustard

1/2 teaspoon Worcestershire sauce

One 4½-ounce can crabmeat

1/2 large unpeeled English hothouse
cucumber

8 pimiento-stuffed green olives, sliced

● ● ● ● ● ● ● ● ● ● ● ● ●

In a small bowl, mix the mayonnaise, horse-radish, mustard, Worcestershire sauce, and crabmeat. Cover and refrigerate for 30 minutes. In the meantime, scrub and dry the cucumber—don't peel—and slice crosswise into 16 thick rounds. (Before slicing, you may want to use a fork to create decorative lines down the side of the cucumber.) Arrange the cucumber slices in a single layer on a serving tray, and spoon 1 tablespoon of the crab mixture onto each slice. Garnish with olive slices and serve. Makes 16 appetizers

A little exotic and very tasty, these crab-topped cucumber rounds will be a refreshing addition to your appetizer buffet. If you can't find crab, or don't like it, just substitute a similar size can of tuna, chicken, or turkey.

Simple Idea

For a delicious and elegant beverage, serve sparkling white pear juice in a tall chilled glass with frozen white grapes and a mint leaf—a memorable drink for a memorable evening.

Snappy Appetizer Tray

The wonder of this appetizer tray is that most of it can be found in a jar or can on your grocer's shelf. Some items are found in the pickles-and-olives aisle; others are by the gourmet cheese case. They'll keep easily in your pantry, ready for last-minute hospitality.

Making It Beautiful

The real key to presenting appetizers beautifully is a liberal and creative use of greenery. Don't limit yourself to plain old lettuce. Try kale for a beautiful frilly effect. Banana leaves are great if you can find them (try a florist)—they provide a nice flat background and hold up well throughout the evening. I love to garnish with rosemary at Christmastime because it looks like little pine branches. You can also use edible unsprayed flowers such as pansies, baby-sized fruits such as kumquats or key or Mexican limes, large cinnamon sticks tied together, and unshelled nuts in a variety of shapes and colors. Don't forget the bounty of the outdoors—use Christmas greenery under punch bowls or to garland your platters. But be sure that all garnishes are edible or at least non toxic.

Salad greens for garnish—try arugula; red leaf, Boston, or Bibb lettuce; mustard greens or kale; or fresh basil leaves

1 jar or can each of baby corn on the cob, sweet pickles, pepperoncini, marinated sweet red peppers, cherry peppers, marinated carrot sticks, marinated artichoke hearts, pitted Kalamata olives, pitted green olives, capers

3 kinds of cheese, such as brie (a 4-ounce wedge), sharp cheddar (a 4-ounce chunk), and goat cheese with jalapeno (a 4-ounce chunk)

Fresh sliced salami

Green onions, (scallions) with the root ends cut off

Cherry or grape tomatoes

Crackers of your choice

• •

Place a plastic storage container upside down in the center of a large tray. Wash the greens, tear from the base into large leaves, and use to cover both the tray and the container. Open the jars of pickled items and arrange in clusters on the tray, saving half the jar of sweet pickles. Place the cheeses in the center of the tray on top of the greens-covered storage container, along with a small cheese knife. Roll up some of the sweet pickles in salami slices, 1 pickle per salami slice, and place these in little stacks in three or four areas on the tray. Finally, group green onions and cherry tomatoes around the tray.

Place crackers in a basket or on a separate plate or tray. Display your appetizer tray and accompanying crackers on the kitchen counter or dining table and allow it to entice your guests to partake. Makes at least 20 appetizer servings

One Cheese Ball, Five Ways

One 8-ounce package cream cheese, softened

½ cup milk

2¼ cups shredded sharp cheddar cheese

¼ cup chopped green onions (scallions), green and white parts

1 cup chopped almonds, walnuts, or pecans

Salt and freshly ground black pepper

¼ cup chopped fresh parsley and other fresh herbs such as basil or thyme

• • • • • • • • • • • • • • •

Beat together the cream cheese and milk until smooth. Add the shredded cheese, green onions, and half of the nuts. Mix well and season with salt and pepper. Transfer the mixture to a large piece of plastic wrap and form into a ball. Wrap tightly and chill at least 2 hours. In a pie plate, mix the parsley and the remaining chopped nuts. Unwrap the chilled cheese ball and gently roll it in the nut-parsley mixture. Wrap again in a clean piece of plastic wrap and chill up to 24 hours. Makes 10 to 12 appetizer servings

Beautiful, easy, and oh, so versatile! You must try the pineapple variation. My friend Leanna Tuff introduced me to it, and it is amazing.

Simple Variations

Savory Treat Substitute ¼ cup crumbled blue cheese for ¼ cup of the cheddar, use pecans for the nuts, and add 5 slices crumbled crisp-cooked, bacon to the cheese mixture. Add 5 more slices crumbled bacon to the nut-parsley mixture for rolling.

Spice It Up Add ½ teaspoon minced garlic, 1 tablespoon Worcestershire sauce, and 1 tablespoon hot pepper sauce. Roll in a mixture of nuts, parsley, paprika, and chili powder.

Pineapple Delight Omit the milk. Substitute white cheddar for the cheese and add ¾ cup crushed pineapple in heavy syrup (undrained), ½ each large red and green bell pepper, finely chopped and 2 tablespoons seasoned salt (I prefer Lawry's.) Roll in crushed almonds, cashews, or macadamia nuts.

Seafood Special Omit the milk, green onions, and nuts. Instead of regular cheddar cheese, use ½ cup shredded white sharp cheddar with jalapeños. Add 2 pounds shredded crabmeat (imitation crab works fine), 2 finely chopped medium yellow onions, 2 cups finely chopped celery, ½ teaspoon garlic powder, 2 tablespoons Worcestershire sauce, 1 teaspoon seasoned salt (preferably Lawry's) and ½ teaspoon freshly cracked pepper. Roll the ball in parsley only and pour bottled cocktail sauce over the chilled ball.

Simple Idea

For a truly spectacular cheese ball presentation, pat your favorite cheese ball recipe into a pinecone shape, kind of a flattened oval with one pointed end. Beginning at the pointed end, cover with whole toasted almonds, working your way to the other end. Garnish with rosemary twigs or well-washed evergreen sprigs and pinecones.

Festive Cream Cheese Tree

Two 8-ounce packages cream cheese, softened

One 7-ounce jar basil (green) pesto

One 7-ounce jar marinated sun-dried tomatoes, drained well and sliced into thin strips

Lemon peel and kale or Bibb lettuce for garnish (optional)

Crackers, for serving

This is another super-easy appetizer. I have a friend who makes this for parties and charges a hundred dollars for it!

On a plate or platter, form the cream cheese into a Christmas tree shape. "Frost" the cream cheese with the pesto and decorate with the sun-dried tomatoes. If you wish, you can top your tree with a star cut from lemon peel and make a tree skirt out of kale or Bibb lettuce. Or you can form the cream cheese into the shape of a wreath, bell, or topiary plant. Use your creativity and imagination. Serve with your favorite crackers. Makes 12 to 16 appetizer servings

Coconut Angel Cupcakes

Beautiful, delectable, and deliciously bite-size, these heavenly mini cupcakes are perfect for an appetizer buffet.

A Simply Smashing Presentation

Serving small treats like cupcakes, petit fours, chocolates, and small cookies on a tiered tray saves a lot of space and makes a beautiful statement. Look for pretty little trays in thrift stores, outlets, and antique stores. Or make your own multitiered server by stacking glass circles or round mirrors (from a hobby store or glass store) with some kind of separator. For a small "tree" to serve mini cupcakes or petit fours, stack 12-inch, 10-inch, 8-inch, and 6-inch circles on two different sizes of glass bowls or custard cups (open side up). For a table-size display, use glass hurricanes to support larger glass circles. The lower levels will need 3 to 4 hurricanes each, depending on the size and weight of your glass circles. Place them at clock positions around the perimeter and fill with flowers, greenery, or small fruit such as kumquats, tiny apples, or cranberries before placing a circle on top.

2 cups sweetened flaked coconut

1 box white cake mix (the kind with pudding added)

1 small box (3.4 ounce or 4-serving size) vanilla instant pudding mix

1 small box (3.4 ounce or 4-serving size) coconut cream instant pudding mix (or another box of vanilla)

4 large eggs, lightly beaten

1½ cup canned coconut milk (not cream of coconut)

½ cup vegetable oil

2 teaspoons coconut extract

1 cup chopped nuts (optional)

Silver or gold mini cupcake liners

Store-bought vanilla frosting or Easy Cream Cheese Frosting (page 23) made with 1 teaspoon coconut extract and 1 teaspoon almond extract

· ·

Preheat the oven to 350°F. Spread 1 cup of the coconut on a baking sheet and toast until golden. Set aside to cool. Combine the cake mix, pudding mixes, eggs, coconut milk, oil, the remaining coconut, the coconut extract, and nuts, if using. Mix by hand for 50 strokes, or about 20 seconds with an electric mixer. (Some mix may remain only partially blended.) Pour into miniature cupcake pans lined with silver or gold baking cups and bake 12 to 15 minutes, until tops spring back when lightly touched. Transfer the cupcakes to a wire rack and cool to room temperature. Top each with a swirl of frosting and sprinkle with toasted coconut. Makes about 24 mini cupcakes

Chapter 9

No Place Like Home

Fun and delicious time-out evenings

Whatever else you do this holiday season—whatever parties you attend (or throw), whatever activities you pursue—try to reserve at least one evening at home. One evening when you and the ones you love aren't scheduled for anything else. One evening when you're all there together, enjoying the lighted tree, nibbling great snacks from the Christmas Kitchen . . . just being together. One warm, delightful, cozy evening with the people you love most.

But note that I didn't say "quiet evening."

I have four older kids and a little grandson living with me, and their friends are often here at the house as well. That means our evenings together are seldom quiet. Sometimes they're downright rambunctious, with everyone talking at once, lots of laughter, the baby shrieking in glee or indignation, and even the occasional argument.

That's just what it's like at my house when everyone's home—and I love it, because even with the noise, there's still something peaceful about us all being together. About gathering together in one room, munching on holiday goodies, not having to be anywhere but home. There's something restorative about having a time-out from the holiday rush, a respite from busyness.

Such an evening might be quiet, of course. It depends on who you are, what you like to do, the size of your household, and the ages of all involved. If you live alone, you might enjoy a silent evening in your pajamas with a good book and a new CD of carols. (Boy, does that sound nice to me right about now!) You might invite a friend or two over for snacks or a simple dinner. (Nothing wrong with importing a few folks to share your evening at home.) Or you might combine an inexpensive family outing (check your local listings for activities) with a fun time at home before and after.

Whatever activity you choose, it needs to be intentional—you need to plan for it. If your household is anything like mine, if you don't mark that time off on your calendar, your time together won't happen. Something will come up. Someone will make plans. Your evening at home needs to be a definite date, something you prepare for and honor.

You might be worried about getting the rest of your family to stay at home without grumbling . . . especially if you have teenagers or a busy spouse or roommate. And of course it's important to give everyone enough lead time to plan their schedules around the evening. But I've found that the best strategy is enticement. Keep everyone's needs and desires and preferences in mind. Do things they already like to do. Light a fire in the fireplace. Put on some favorite holiday music—theirs as well as yours. Let them invite some friends over to share your together time. (You'll be giving a gift to the friends as well.)

Best of all, be sure you have some favorite food treats on hand. (If you feed them, they will come.) It doesn't have to be fancy. Pizza for dinner almost always hits the spot—and it doesn't have to be homemade. A fabulous dip or appetizer is always welcome. A frozen dessert can be especially delicious in front of a blazing fire. And always, always have popcorn on hand.

If something comes up and somebody in the house can't be there, don't let it derail you—resolve to make the most of your evening as it is. You can still enjoy your respite with someone missing. Even if you make a mistake in the scheduling and nobody's home but you, determine to enjoy your now-quiet evening.

It's good to have a bit of a game plan, an inkling of what you're going to do together, even if it's just sitting on the couch and watching a Christmas special on TV. One of our favorite family activities during the holiday season is popping a big bowl of popcorn and watching *A Charlie Brown Christmas* together. In earlier years, when my children were younger, we often played games or worked on crafts. Some years we've spent the time in the kitchen together, making snacks or working together on edible gifts and make-ahead meals—and talking a mile a minute while we cooked.

It doesn't really matter what you do. What matters is taking a break from the hectic pace of the holiday season, giving everybody time to catch their breath. What matters is enjoying each other, being thankful for one another, showing true hospitality to one another . . . and remembering that there's really no place like home for the holidays.

Spicy Nut Mix

Nonstick cooking spray

3 tablespoons unsalted butter, melted

1 tablespoon hot sauce

1 tablespoon ground cumin

1 teaspoon chili powder

½ teaspoon garlic powder

¼ cup plus 1 tablespoon bottled chili sauce

2 tablespoons frozen orange juice concentrate, thawed

2 cups raw pecan halves

1 cup raw or roasted cashews, preferably unsalted

1 cup hot-and-spicy peanuts or plain dryroasted peanuts

1 cup shelled roasted pistachios

½ cup pine nuts

This delicious mix is perfect for an evening at home, and it's also a tasty addition to gift baskets.

Preheat the oven to 300°F. Spray two large cookie sheets or jelly-roll pans with nonstick spray. In a large bowl, combine the butter, hot sauce, cumin, chili powder, garlic powder, chili sauce, and orange juice. Add all the nuts and stir to coat thoroughly. Spread the nut mixture in a single layer on the cookie sheets and bake about 20 minutes, stirring occasionally, until nuts are crisp and lightly browned. (They burn easily, so watch them.) Let cool and store in a covered container. Makes 5 ½ cups

The Maltbys' Famous Spinach-Artichoke Dip

*Here's our family's special take on a favorite dip.
Everyone loves it. Serve with sliced bell peppers
(red, green, and yellow), carrots, celery, crackers,
chips, or homemade pita crisps (see below).*

Simple Idea

To make ahead, prepare the dip mixture, place in the pan, cover, and refrigerate for up to 24 hours. When ready to bake, place in a cold oven, set it to 400°F, and bake about 45 minutes.

Simple Idea

To make pita crisps, cut 6 pita bread rounds in half horizontally, separate the layers, and cut each half into 6 wedges. Place the pita wedges in a single layer on an ungreased cookie sheet, spray with olive oil cooking spray, and sprinkle with garlic salt and freshly ground black pepper. Bake uncovered in a 350°F oven for 10 to 12 minutes, until crisp. You can bake these ahead and store in a plastic bag for up to 24 hours or freeze up to 2 weeks. Reheat in the oven until warm. Makes 72 wedges.

• •

Preheat the oven to 400°F. Mix together all ingredients up to cilantro. Season to taste with salt, pepper, and hot sauce. (I use about 4 shakes). Spray a 2-quart baking dish or 13 by 9-inch baking pan generously with nonstick spray. Pour in the dip and bake for 35 minutes, or until hot and bubbly. Makes about 12 generous appetizer servings

Three 14-ounce cans artichoke hearts, drained and chopped

One 10- to 14.5-ounce can diced tomatoes with green chiles (such as Rotel), drained well

One 8-ounce package cream cheese, softened

1 cup sour cream (low-fat is fine)

1 cup mayonnaise-type salad dressing such as Miracle Whip (low-fat is fine)

½ cup drained and chopped oil-packed sun-dried tomatoes

4 cups shredded pepper Jack cheese

1 cup shredded Parmesan cheese

One 10-ounce box frozen chopped spinach, thawed and drained well

½ cup chopped green onions (scallions), white and green parts

2 teaspoons minced garlic

½ cup chopped cilantro or parsley

Bottled hot sauce

Salt and pepper

Nonstick cooking spray

Teddy Bear Caramel Corn

1 cup packed light-brown sugar

½ cup (1 stick) salted butter

½ cup light corn syrup

½ teaspoon baking soda

6 quarts popped popcorn, salted, with unpopped kernels removed (microwave popcorn works fine)

2 cups small cinnamon-flavored, bear-shaped graham-cracker snacks (such as Teddy Grahams)

• • • • • • • • • • • • • • • •

Combine the sugar, butter, and syrup in an 8-cup microwave-safe container. Microwave on HIGH until the butter melts, then stir. Microwave another minute or so on HIGH, until mixture comes to a boil, then boil for 1½ minutes. Stir again and boil 30 seconds more to make a syrup. (You might need to adjust these times, depending on the strength of your microwave.) Remove from the oven and add the baking soda, stirring quickly. Watch that the mixture doesn't boil over. Pour over the popcorn in a large clean paper grocery bag, fold over top of bag, and shake vigorously to distribute syrup. Microwave the bag 1½ minutes on HIGH and shake again. Microwave 30 seconds more, add graham crackers, and shake. Spread the mixture out onto parchment or waxed paper and cool. Store in an airtight container. Makes about 7 quarts

This caramel popcorn is easy to make, a welcome gift, and perfect for Christmas movie night. If you wish, you can make popcorn balls out of this mixture. Just butter your hands or spray them with cooking spray and shape into balls instead of spreading the mixture out to cool. Because the syrup gets hot, this is not an activity for small or unsupervised kids.

Simple Variation

For a spicy treat, add a handful of small red cinnamon candies along with the graham crackers. You can also substitute 1 cup of salted cashews or peanuts or 1 cup toasted almonds or pecans for the bears.

Pear, Brie, and Smoked Turkey Bruschetta

This has become my family's favorite snack. You can change the meat to prosciutto, add a little crumbled blue cheese to the Brie, swap the fruit to a Fuji or Granny Smith apple, and use snipped rosemary instead of basil. Fresh herbs in this recipe make all the difference!

One 4½-ounce round Brie or other white, soft cheese, well chilled

Sixteen ¼-inch-thick slices French bread

1 tablespoon melted salted or unsalted butter or olive oil

4 ounces thinly sliced smoked turkey, cut in 2-inch pieces

1 soft medium pear, cored and cut into 16 slices (no need to peel)

1 tablespoon finely snipped fresh basil, (or as much as desired)

Remove rind from the Brie if you desire and cut round into 16 wedges. Place the bread slices on a cookie sheet and broil about 6 inches from heat for 1 to 2 minutes, until lightly toasted. Turn the slices over. Brush the tops lightly with the melted butter and broil 1 to 2 minutes more. Remove from the oven. Divide the turkey, pear, and Brie among the toasted bread slices. Sprinkle with basil. Broil for 2 minutes more or until cheese begins to soften. Serve warm. Makes 16 appetizer servings

Joyful Java Ice Cream Dessert

One 11-ounce loaf angel food cake or a regular-size round angel food cake

1 tablespoon dark-roast instant coffee granules

1 tablespoon hot water

2 teaspoons vanilla extract

1 teaspoon almond extract

4½ cups chocolate chip ice cream, softened

Four 1.4-ounce chocolate-covered toffee candy bars such as Heath, crushed, or ¾ cup milk chocolate toffee bits

3 tablespoons coffee-mocha syrup such as Entner-Stuart Café Mocha Trio

One 8-ounce tub of extra-creamy whipped topping such as Cool Whip thawed

This delicious cold dessert is perfect for eating by a warm fire on a family evening—and stays ready in your freezer for impromptu family parties. If you don't have a spring-form pan, you can use a 13 by 9-inch baking pan and cut the finished dessert into squares.

Cut the cake into ½-inch slices. Arrange the cake slices, overlapping, in bottom of a 9-inch springform pan (you should have leftover cake) and set aside. Combine the coffee granules, hot water, vanilla extract, and almond extract in a medium bowl. Stir well. Stir in the ice cream and crushed candy. Spread the ice cream mixture over the cake slices. Gently stir the syrup into the whipped topping and spread over ice cream. Cover with aluminum foil and freeze for at least 8 hours (overnight is even better). Unmold. Dip a knife in warm water to cut into slices and serve. Makes 12 servings

Simple Variation

The ice cream and toffee mixture makes a wonderful ice cream sandwich, too. Just spread the softened ice cream between large cookies of your choice, wrap in plastic wrap, and freeze until firm.

Simple Hint

Café Mocha Trio is a syrup used at many coffee shops (ask if they'll sell you a shot) and available online as well. If you can't find it anywhere, try mixing 1 teaspoon chocolate syrup, 1 teaspoon dark-roast instant coffee granules, and 2 tablespoons water or 1 teaspoon chocolate syrup and 2 tablespoons strong brewed coffee or espresso. Stir together well.

Ideas for Fun Family Evenings

❋ Watch a movie or Christmas TV special. Be sure to include for consideration shows that are not technically about Christmas but have Christmas as part of the storyline— *It's a Wonderful Life*, *Meet Me in St. Louis*, even *Sleepless in Seattle*. Another wonderful possibility is to watch old family Christmas videos, DVDs, or even home movies if you have them. (This might be a great time to have those old media digitized and preserved.) Your whole family will be on the floor laughing at the images of themselves from an earlier time.

❋ A weekend afternoon outing can sub for an at-home evening. Visit a Christmas tree farm, treat yourself to a carriage ride, or go caroling, then enjoy at-home snacks and some cozy downtime.

❋ Have a traveling Christmas pajama party. This is great for times when the budget is tight. Pack up a car picnic of hot cocoa (in thermoses), popcorn, cookies, or other treats. Get the kids bathed and ready for bed, in PJs and slippers. Then pile into the car, put classic Christmas carols on the stereo, and drive around to look at Christmas lights.

❋ Research Christmas customs in another culture and try making some food or craft that reflects those customs. Even better, invite someone from another country over to tell you about Christmas in his or her homeland. We did this when Viviana, a young woman from Mexico, was living with us. It was a blast—she taught us a lot about having a Mexican Christmas!

❄ Make gifts. If your kids are little, this is a great time to bring out the paint, glitter, macaroni, modeling clay—whatever!—and make presents for grandparents. For a much-appreciated gift, have kids write (or dictate) their favorite memory with a grandparent and draw pictures to illustrate it. Older kids might want to do the same thing using several memories, photographs, and computer graphics. You can even use your computer to make gift calendars with photos of the kids with their grandparents.

❄ Read a Christmas book or story aloud, with everyone taking turns reading.

Chapter 10

Just Like We Always Do

Traditions old and new for a joyful Christmas Eve

T is the night (and the day) before Christmas . . . and things are really cooking in the Christmas Kitchen.

There's always last-minute shopping. (No matter how carefully I plan, it seems I always forget something.) There's prep for tomorrow's breakfast and dinner, and there are goodies to prepare for tonight.

In our house, at least, Christmas Eve is as big an occasion as Christmas itself.

I grew up in a big family with Scandinavian roots, and for us, the night before Christmas was always family time. We would attend an early candlelit church service, then come home to eat and enjoy a Nativity play by the kids. (As the youngest, I had no choice of roles—I was *always* Baby Jesus.) We noshed on special snacks served only on this special day: Christmas pudding, nuts in a bowl with a nutcracker, or my mama's round butter cookies coated with sugar. And then we opened our presents, one at a time, with everyone watching the papers fall off every gift and oohing and aahing—and saying thank you—over each one.

That was our family tradition, and it has continued to be so. And that's important, because if ever there was a time for tradition, it's Christmas Eve and Christmas Day.

Some of our traditions have changed a little over the years, though, and I'm sure yours have, too. If you're married, you've probably had to reach a compromise or two about what to do and when (Christmas Eve or Christmas morning, travel or stay home, your parents' house or your spouse's). If you have kids, you've adjusted the schedule and the activities as they grew. And chances are, you've picked up a new tradition along the way for the night before Christmas. A special book to "always" read. A new carol to "always" sing. Activities to "always" enjoy, like lighting the last Advent candle or putting on a pageant or strolling around the neighborhood to see the lights. And of course special new offerings from the Christmas Kitchen that quickly become a treasured part of the night-before-Christmas ritual.

One of our favorite new/old traditions is a Christmas Eve supper that reflects both my Scandinavian roots (a divine rice pudding) and our years in Texas (cranberry-studded guacamole and spicy tortilla soup). Mexican food was not a part of my growing up in Minnesota, but to my family now, it wouldn't be Christmas without it. My kids are almost grown, and my only grandson is still a toddler, so we probably won't have a children's play—that's a tradition that might have to wait a bit to be revived. But we still go into the living room to open our presents one at a time, while everyone watches. (My kids still laugh about the year I mixed up all their gift tags in my attempt to be clever.) And through the seasons of our lives, as Christmases come and go, we wouldn't have it any other way.

What are the Christmas Eve traditions that your Christmas Kitchen supports? Enjoy them, cherish them, repeat them . . . but hold them lightly, because more is yet to come, with new joys to be found in the unfolding of the years.

If Santa Claus comes to your house, the Christmas Kitchen might provide traditional cookies to leave with a note . . . but maybe this year you'll leave delicious cool-mint cookies or some granola for the reindeer. If your family doesn't do the Santa thing, or if the kids are too old this year, why not let them camp out under the Christmas tree for the night? (My children dearly loved this tradition.) If your church offers a midnight service to attend, maybe this is the year your kids are old enough to stay up for it. And perhaps you'll find something new and delicious to send you on your way or settle you back down when you return.

That's the beauty of the Christmas season: It's timeless and fresh, traditional yet flexible. Not really bound by space and time, yet held tightly in the embrace of memory.

Something always old, something ever new . . . and to all a beautiful, holy, and delicious good night.

Feliz Navidad Tortilla Soup

1 quart chicken broth

3 whole skinless chicken breasts (about 2 pounds total)

½ cup chopped yellow onion

1 teaspoon ground cumin

1 clove garlic, minced

Vegetable oil

One 14½-ounce can diced tomatoes

One 8-ounce can tomato sauce

One 4-ounce can diced green chiles (double this amount if you like)

½ cup snipped fresh cilantro (my preference) or parsley

2 tablespoons snipped fresh oregano or 2 teaspoons dried, crushed

Six 5½-inch corn tortillas

1½ cups shredded cheddar or pepper Jack cheese

One 8-ounce container of low-fat sour cream

1 Hass avocado, seeded, peeled, and cubed

This is a real family favorite—I've made it every Christmas for at least fifteen years, starting when we lived in Texas, and carried the tradition on to our current Colorado home. Now my daughter Mackenzie is marrying a young man with a Mexican heritage, and he loves it, so this tradition is one we'll continue for years to come.

Simple Hint

I always double the recipe for this soup. It freezes wonderfully and is always an appreciated gift. I like to freeze 2 to 3 cup servings (a great lunch!) in reusable plastic containers.

• •

Pour the broth into a large saucepan or Dutch oven. Add the chicken and bring to a boil. Reduce the heat and simmer, covered, about 15 minutes or until chicken is tender and no longer pink. Remove the chicken from the broth and reserve the broth separately. Let stand until cool enough to handle. Remove and discard the bones. Finely shred the chicken and set aside.

In same saucepan, cook onion, cumin, and garlic in 1 tablespoon hot oil until onion is tender but not brown. Stir in the broth, undrained tomatoes, tomato sauce, chiles, cilantro, and oregano. Bring to a boil, then reduce heat and simmer, covered, for 20 minutes. Stir in the chicken and heat through.

Cut tortillas in half, then cut them crosswise into ½-inch strips. In a heavy medium skillet, heat ¼ inch vegetable oil. Fry the tortilla strips in the hot oil, half at a time, about 1 minute or until crisp and light brown. Remove with a slotted spoon and drain on paper towels.

Divide the tortilla strips among six bowls. Ladle the soup over the tortilla strips. Sprinkle each serving with pepper Jack cheese, a spoonful of sour cream, and cubes of avocado. Serve immediately. Makes 6 hearty servings

Cranberry Guacamole

I was a guest on a TV show years ago and watched a chef whip up this special holiday version of one of my favorites. I think I ate the whole bowl by myself! Since then, I've changed it up to suit my own tastes. I love the Christmasy colors as well as the spectacular taste.

Simple Idea

If time is really short, just buy commercial guacamole and add the cranberries to it with a squeeze of lime juice to freshen the taste.

Simple Idea

Make your own chips by cutting flavored flour tortillas into wedges. Or use a cookie cutter to cut out shapes from pesto-flavored (green) and sun-dried-tomato-flavored (red) tortillas. Brush with olive oil, sprinkle with garlic salt and ground cumin, and bake at 350°F until crisp.

1 cup dried sweetened cranberries (such as Craisins) or dried cherries

3 ripe Hass avocados, seeded and peeled

½ cup canned or bottled salsa verde (green salsa)

¼ cup chopped fresh cilantro or parsley leaves

1 fresh jalapeño, seeded and finely chopped

1 teaspoon coarse garlic salt

Juice of 1 large lime

• • • • • • • • • • • • • • • • • •

Soak the cranberries in cold water for 10 minutes. Drain and squeeze dry. Coarsely mash avocados and fold in the cranberries, salsa, cilantro, jalapeño, garlic salt, and lime juice. Guacamole is best made as close to serving as possible. For short-term storage, seal in an airtight container with a piece of plastic wrap pressed against the surface of the guacamole. Serve with tortilla chips—red and green if available. Makes about 12 average servings—or 6 for me (I love guacamole!)

Santa's Favorite Faux Thin Mints

One 10-ounce package chocolate-mint
baking chips, such as Andes Crème-de-
Menthe chips

One 16-ounce package low-sodium buttery
crackers, such as Ritz

White chocolate chips, crushed peppermint
pieces, red and green sprinkles (optional)

. . . .

Place a large cookie sheet in your freezer
for about 15 minutes. While it cools, place
the crème-de-menthe in a microwave-safe
baking container. Melt carefully on HIGH,
30 seconds at a time, stirring after each 30
seconds. Remove the cookie sheet from the
freezer and cover with waxed paper or parchment paper. Using two forks, dip each cracker
in the melted chocolate to coat completely.
Place on the cookie sheet. Wipe away any
chocolate that spreads around the cookie,
but the cold cookie sheet should keep it from
spreading. If necessary, put the cookie sheet
back in the freezer for a few minutes to keep
it cold. If you wish, decorate the cookies with
squiggles of melted white chocolate (melt
the white chocolate chips just as you did the
mint ones), crushed peppermint, or sprinkles.
Makes about 4 dozen cookies

If you (or Santa) have a taste for a certain kind of Girl Scout cookie, you've got to try these. They're unbelievably easy and delicious—and taste just like the real thing. You can make as few or as many as you like.

Simple Hint

I find the crème-de-menthe chips easiest to work with for this recipe. If you can't find them, just follow the directions on page 128 for melting dark or milk chocolate, then flavor to taste with peppermint oil (I use about 5 drops). Alternatives for the butter crackers are vanilla wafers, chocolate graham crackers, or best of all—if you can find them—chocolate wafers such as Nabisco's Famous Chocolate Wafers.

To Make Your Christmas a Little Simpler

Christmas Eve morning is a great time to sit down and go through all your Christmas plans and recipes one more time. Do you have all the ingredients on hand? Will you need extra ice? Is there enough butter to make gravy and still set some out on the table? Do you need an extra pie just in case? Are all your serving dishes clean and ready? Do you need to iron a tablecloth? If your dining table is free, why not go ahead and set it for Christmas dinner—or set the dining room table for Christmas Eve and the kitchen table for Christmas morning breakfast. (I love to put a Nativity set in the middle of my table for Christmas morning.) Even better, assign your kids the job of setting the table, making centerpieces, and writing out name tags.

Make as much of your Christmas Day breakfast as you can on Christmas Eve morning. I always do this with my Christmas Morning Cinnamon Wreath (page 112). Right before I go to bed on Christmas Eve, I make the wreath and let it rise at room temperature so it's ready to bake on Christmas morning. (Cover with plastic wrap sprayed with cooking spray so it doesn't stick to the wreath.) Blueberries for Brunch (page 72) is also easy to make Christmas Eve night, refrigerate, and slip into the oven on Christmas morning to bake.

Lost-and-Found Rice Pudding

½ cup (1 stick) unsalted butter (not margarine), plus more for the baking dish

2 quarts whole milk

1 cup jasmine rice

1 cup golden raisins

8 large eggs, beaten

2/3 cup granulated sugar

1 tablespoon vanilla extract

1 teaspoon salt

Ground cinnamon, nutmeg, or allspice

Fresh whipped cream or half-and-half

The top of this pudding is custard, the rice settles to the bottom, and the whole thing is amazingly yummy—definitely not low-calorie, but worth the splurge. We lost this recipe for almost eight years and tried about twenty-five other rice pudding recipes but could never get it as creamy and delicious. While working on this book, I went through all my recipes and books—no small task—and found it. That night we made a double batch and ate it all!

• •

Preheat the oven to 325°F. Generously butter a 3-quart baking dish. In a heavy 4-quart saucepan, combine 1 quart of the milk with the rice and the raisins. Bring to a full boil. Quickly reduce heat, cover, and cook over very low heat until rice is tender, about 15 minutes. Stir several times and watch carefully to prevent boilovers. When rice is fully cooked, remove from the heat and stir in the butter until melted. In a large bowl, combine remaining milk, the eggs, sugar, vanilla, and salt; gradually stir into the cooked rice. Pour into the prepared baking dish. Bake uncovered for 30 minutes. Stir and sprinkle with cinnamon, nutmeg, or allspice. (I generally use two of the three.) Return to the oven and bake another 25 minutes or until edges are set. The center will still be jiggly. Let sit 10 minutes. Serve with fresh whipped cream or half-and-half. Makes 12 servings

Chapter 11

Always Room at Our Table

Cooking up a fun and festive Christmas Day

Today the Christmas Kitchen is in its glory!

First, it supplies something wonderful for waking up . . . coffee to sip at the crack of dawn, savory cinnamon rolls for munching while children check their stockings, maybe something more substantial (scrambled eggs, anyone?) for sustenance while your family's Christmas morning gets underway.

Perhaps you hear squeals of delight as little ones discover what Santa has left.

Perhaps your morning begins with a gentle stirring as teens or housemates gradually awaken to the big day.

Maybe there's a scurry to get ready for church.

Or your Christmas Kitchen might welcome the excitement of one relative or friend after another arriving—big hugs, warm greetings, gifts changing hands.

No matter what the morning holds, eventually the preparation for Christmas dinner must begin.

It's the best meal of the year . . . and I believe it's meant to be shared. With family of course, and I've always had a big one. But even if your household is tiny, I urge you to approach Christmas dinner with a spirit of "the more the merrier."

Open your eyes: The possibilities for sharing the best meal of the year are endless. Look for students who can't go home, young people on their own, single parents and their kids—anyone in need of a little extended family. Or if you happen to be at loose ends yourself, make a point to join forces with others for a Christmas Kitchen extravaganza—a lavish potluck or a shared kitchen.

Don't forget to share the preparation—that's part of the fun, too. The joys of the Christmas Kitchen begin long before the loaded platters reach the table, and as the saying goes, many hands make light work. In fact, I urge you to include a game plan for delegating tasks as part of your Christmas-morning strategy. One person can peel potatoes, another can cut up broccoli, someone can whip cream, and guests can bring their own specialties to share. Even the littlest ones can put ice in glasses or carry coats to the spare bedroom.

Then, finally, the moment comes: It's dinnertime.

Time to light the candles, to carry in the beautiful platter of beef or turkey or ham. Time to join hands around the table, look into each other's eyes, and offer a prayer of gratitude.

Not just for dinner but for a year full of blessings.

Not just for the joy of gathering together but for the gift of one another.

And most of all, for what this celebration signifies.

That Love has come into the world.

That God is truly with us.

And that heaven and nature—and all of us who gather in the Christmas Kitchen—are singing joyfully together.

Christmas Morning Cinnamon Wreath

Shortening or nonstick cooking spray

Two 1-pound loaves frozen bread dough, thawed in the refrigerator overnight

¼ cup (½ stick) unsalted butter, softened

1 cup packed light-brown sugar

¼ cup granulated sugar

Ground cinnamon

½ cup chopped Granny Smith apple

¼ cup raisins

1 tablespoon grated lemon or orange peel

2 cups confectioners' sugar

Milk

1 small jar red maraschino cherries, drained

1 small jar green maraschino cherries, drained

Greens, for presentation

I love this recipe because it's easy yet looks like it took a lot of work. Don't you just love that?

Heat the oven to 200°F and then turn it off. Grease a cookie sheet with shortening or cooking spray and set aside. Combine the 2 pieces of dough and roll out to a rectangle about 20 by 14 inches. Spread the dough with the butter and sprinkle evenly with the brown and granulated sugars. Shake cinnamon liberally over the entire surface, then spread the apple, raisins, and citrus peel evenly on top. Roll up the dough from the long side and pinch the ends to seal.

To make the wreath, take the roll and press the ends together to make a circle. Make cuts halfway through the dough all around the circle, leaving the dough in the center intact. Place the dough circle on the cookie sheet and flip each cut section on its side so the whole thing looks like a big wreath. Put in the still-warm oven to let dough rise, or let rise at room temperature overnight (see page 105). When the dough has doubled in size, about 30 minutes in the warm oven, remove it from the oven and preheat the oven to 350°F. Return the wreath to oven and bake 25 minutes, until light brown. Let cool slightly, then carefully loosen the wreath with a spatula and slide it onto a large platter. Mix the confectioners' sugar with enough milk to make a thin icing and drizzle over the wreath. Add clusters of red and green cherries to the wreath (like ornaments). Finish the presentation with some Christmas greens around the platter. Serve warm. Makes 12 generous servings

Simple Variations

This recipe works just as well for cinnamon rolls. After rolling up dough, slice evenly into 12 pieces. Space evenly in a greased 13 by 9-inch baking pan. Let rise and bake as for cinnamon wreath. Drizzle icing over the rolls and serve warm.

In place of the apples and raisins, use just ½ cup raisins; ½ cup dried, sweetened cranberries or cherries; or ½ cup dried apricots, snipped into pieces. If you use apricots, use apricot nectar to mix the frosting—yum!

Even simpler: use 2 cans of refrigerator cinnamon rolls and place in a circle, slightly overlapping, on the cookie sheet. Bake as directed on the package, ice, and decorate as above.

For a Christmas evening treat, make a savory wreath: Prepare the dough as above, but replace the butter with extra virgin olive oil. In place of the sugars, cinnamon, and fruit, use similar amounts of grated Parmesan cheese, chopped sun-dried tomatoes or roasted red peppers (from a jar), and chopped fresh herbs such as basil and oregano. After wreath has risen, brush with olive oil and sprinkle with more Parmesan and herbs. Bake as above. (Skip the icing on this one.) Decorate with more tomatoes or red peppers and sprigs of fresh herbs.

Chilled Cranberry Soup

4 cups fresh cranberries

3 cups water

1½ cups sugar

One 4-inch cinnamon stick

¼ teaspoon ground cloves

½ teaspoon ground allspice

2 tablespoons lemon juice

1 tablespoon finely shredded lemon peel

1 tablespoon finely shredded orange peel

Two 11-ounce cans mandarin oranges, drained

Mint leaves for garnish (optional)

I've served this fruity soup to kick off Christmas dinner for many years now. It's cool, refreshing, and festive. Best of all, it can be made days ahead and served directly from the refrigerator.

In a 3-quart saucepan, combine the cranberries, water, sugar, cinnamon, cloves, and allspice and bring to a boil. Reduce heat and simmer uncovered about 5 minutes, or until about half of the cranberries have popped. Remove from the heat. Stir in the lemon juice, lemon peel, orange peel, and half of the mandarin orange sections. Cool. Cover and chill for 4 to 24 hours.

To serve, remove cinnamon stick and ladle soup into bowls. Top each serving with mandarin oranges in star shape with a mint leaf in the center, if desired. Makes 6 to 8 servings

Fit-for-a-King Fillet of Beef

There's no law that says Christmas dinner has to be turkey. This is truly a special-occasion dish, a wonderful alternative for Christmas dinner. I love to serve this meat with old-fashioned buttermilk mashed potatoes, broccoli with a squeeze of lemon or lemon-butter, and the baby carrots flavored with cardamom on page 117. And don't forget dessert: chocolate cake!

● ●

Preheat the oven to 500°F. Pat the fillet dry with paper towels and place in a shallow baking pan. With your hands, spread the butter all over the fillet. Sprinkle with 1 tablespoon salt and the coarsely ground pepper. Roast for 22 minutes for rare, or 25 for medium-rare. (This cut is so tender that it shouldn't be cooked beyond a medium-rare stage.) Remove the beef from the oven and cover tightly with foil. Let the meat rest for 20 minutes, then slice thickly.

To make the sauce, when the beef goes onto the oven, bring the cream to a boil in a large saucepan over medium-high heat. Reduce heat and simmer for 45 to 50 minutes, stirring occasionally, until slightly thickened. While it cooks, soak the sun-dried tomatoes in hot water for 15 minutes. Drain, dry as well as possible with paper towels, and chop. Remove the cream from the heat and add the cheeses, 3/4 teaspoon salt, the ground pepper, and the parsley. Whisk rapidly until the cheeses melt. Fold in the tomatoes and serve with the beef. Recipe makes 8 to 10 servings

1 whole fillet of beef (4 to 5 pounds), trimmed

2 tablespoons (1/4 stick) unsalted butter, softened

Kosher salt

1 tablespoon coarsely ground black pepper

1/2 cup dry-packed sun-dried tomatoes

1 quart heavy cream

1/2 pound Cambozola cheese, chopped, or 3 to 4 ounces Brie, rind removed and chopped

3 tablespoons grated Parmesan cheese

3/4 teaspoon ground black pepper

3 tablespoons minced fresh parsley leaves

Turkey Made Simple

If you prefer turkey to beef for Christmas and you're cooking for a crowd, I suggest buying two birds—a big one and a little one. Roast the larger bird well ahead of time (I actually buy it on sale at Thanksgiving), carve the meat, and freeze in doubled zippered plastic bags to prevent freezer burn—I like to add a little broth to the bags to keep the slices moist. Thaw in the refrigerator and reheat in a covered pan. Roast the smaller bird for a beautiful presentation at the table.

1¼ cups packed dark brown sugar

1/3 cup pineapple juice

1/3 cup honey

Juice and grated peel of half an orange

2 tablespoons Dijon mustard

¼ teaspoon ground cloves

One 8 to 10 pound precooked, presliced ham

Combine the sugar, pineapple juice, honey, orange juice and peel, mustard, and cloves in small sauce pan, bring to a boil, and boil gently until slightly thickened. Layer the ham slices in a 13-by 9-inch baking pan or a slow cooker. Pour the sauce over the ham slices, cover pan, and heat in a 350°F oven for 30 minutes or in the slow cooker on HIGH about an hour. Serves 16

Savory Shortcut Ham

If Christmas wouldn't be Christmas for you without a baked ham, here's a moist and tasty version of the delicious savory ham you love.

Cardamom Carrots

*You are going to love these carrots and make them again
and again. Even picky eaters ask for seconds.*

Simple Idea

Make carrots ahead of time and store them in a zippered plastic
bag. When dinner is almost ready to serve, drop the contents
into a microwave-safe serving bowl and microwave on HIGH
until steamy. Then toss the bag—no mess or clean-up!

• •

Cook the carrots in small amount of boiling water 7 to 8 minutes, until crisp-tender. Drain and
plunge into cold water. (This important step keeps carrots from becoming mushy.) Set aside. Mix
the cornstarch and cooking wine; stir well. Combine the cornstarch mixture, butter, honey, lemon peel, and juices in a large skillet. Stir together over medium heat until the butter melts, then
bring mixture to a boil, stirring constantly. Add the carrots, cardamom, pepper, and salt. Cook,
tossing gently, until mixture is thoroughly heated. Stir in parsley. Makes 6 servings

1½ pounds baby carrots

1 tablespoon cornstarch

1/3 cup dry white cooking wine

½ cup (1 stick) unsalted butter

¼ cup honey

2 teaspoons grated lemon peel

¼ cup lemon juice

¼ cup orange juice

¾ teaspoon ground cardamom

½ teaspoon ground black pepper

¼ teaspoon salt

2 tablespoons chopped fresh parsley

My Mama's Chocolate Cake

2 large eggs

1 cup packed light brown sugar

1 cup granulated sugar

1 cup regular sour cream (not low-fat)

½ teaspoon salt

½ cup unsweetened cocoa powder

2 teaspoons baking soda

2¼ cups all-purpose flour

3 teaspoons vanilla extract or 2 teaspoons vanilla and 1 teaspoon almond

1 cup hot, strong brewed coffee

1 pint (2 cups) heavy cream

1 tablespoon confectioners' sugar

12 to 15 chocolate-dipped strawberries (see page 128)

Fern greens (from a florist)

Cardboard cake circle the same diameter as the layers

I grew up with this delicious cake (the dark cocoa and coffee are key, my mom says)—but the presentation is all my own, and it's spectacular! The strawberries are a splurge in December, but they're worth it. You can also use fresh raspberries or blackberries, chocolate curls, and toasted slivered almonds.

Simple Hint

You can buy clear imitation vanilla to add to whipped cream if you want to keep the cream bright white. Almond extract is also great—my children's favorite. If I use it, I usually add a few slivered almonds to the top.

• •

Preheat the oven to 350°F. Generously grease two 8- or 9-inch round cake pans and line the bottoms with waxed paper or parchment. Beat the eggs in a large bowl with an electric mixer. Add the brown and granulated sugars and beat until smooth. Mix in the sour cream. In separate bowl, stir together the salt, baking soda, and flour. Sift into the egg mixture. Add 2 teaspoons vanilla and the coffee and mix thoroughly. Pour into the prepared pans and bake 25 to 30 minutes or until a toothpick inserted in the center comes out clean. Cool in pans on wire racks for 5 minutes. Run a thin knife around the edges of the layers and turn out onto the racks. Allow to cool completely. While layers cool, put a clean mixing bowl and beaters in the freezer to chill. Pour in the heavy cream and whip until stiff peaks are about to form. Beat in remaining vanilla or the almond extract and the confectioners' sugar until peaks form. Refrigerate until the cake layers are completely cool. (I often put them in my freezer for 10 to 15 minutes to quicken the process.)

To frost the cake, place fern greens on a cake plate. Place the cardboard cake circle on top of the ferns and place one of the cake layers on the circle. (This will prevent the greens from being cut and eaten along with the cake.) Frost the top of the layer generously with whipped cream. Add the second layer and frost the sides and top. Decorate the cake with the chocolate-dipped strawberries. Place any remaining strawberries around the edges of the cake. You can serve it immediately, but chilling the cake for 4 to 6 hours will help set the frosting—and free you for other last-minute tasks. Makes 12 servings

Simple Tips for Orchestrating Stress-Free Christmas Dinner

❄ Choose a menu that can be made ahead as much as possible.

❄ Clean out your refrigerator several days ahead, using up leftovers and throwing away old food to make room for Christmas dishes. If refrigerator space is limited, perhaps a neighbor who is leaving town will let you use his or her fridge. Or if it's cold outside, store food outside, in the garage, or in an unheated storage room. (Be sure to use animal-proof containers.)

❄ Slow cookers are your friend. Many dishes (mashed potatoes, carrots, gravy, even ham or turkey slices) can be made well ahead of time and kept warm in a cooker until serving time. Borrow extras from friends if you need to. Many have removable inserts that can come to the table as serving dishes.

❄ If you weren't able to set the table the day before, do it as early in the day as possible—and delegate the job if you can.

❄ As soon as breakfast is over, get everything ready for after-dinner coffee—water, filter, and coffee in the pot; sugar bowls and creamers filled; teabags ready if you're offering tea as well; cups, saucers, and spoons ready. (For an afternoon or early evening dinner, I simplify things by serving only decaf rather than offering a choice.) When the time comes to serve, ask someone else to distribute the cups and saucers while you start the coffee and prepare to serve dessert.

❄ Run your dishwasher early in the day, hand-wash any remaining dishes, then empty the dishwasher and put all the dishes away. Starting dinner with an empty dishwasher simplifies after-dinner cleanup enormously.

❄ Prepare a list (even if it's just a mental list) of tasks you are willing and able to delegate so that when people ask "What can I do?" you'll know how to answer. Some ideas: taking guests' coats and putting them away, setting the table, lighting candles, filling beverage glasses, transferring food to serving dishes, serving dessert.

❄ Place pitchers of water on or near the table before the meal starts so glasses will be easy to refill. I like to add sliced lemons or oranges and fresh mint to the pitchers—or for a refreshing change, try a combination of sliced cucumbers and citrus.

❄ After dinner, you don't have to clean up everything right away. Put away the leftovers, set the pots to soak, and get the first dishwasher load started, but then linger over dessert, enjoying the glow of yet another beautiful Christmas meal, compliments of the Christmas Kitchen.

Chapter 12

Something New

Enjoying the gentle side of the holidays

Here's a liberating idea: the Christmas Kitchen doesn't have to shut down the morning of December 26.

In fact, did you know that the traditional "Twelve Days of Christmas" actually start on Christmas Day? That's right. The Christmas season was originally supposed to begin on December 25, with the festivities continuing until January 6, the Feast of the Epiphany.

That doesn't mean you have to keep Christmas going full-tilt until January 6, although some people do just that. Personally, by the time Christmas Day is over, I'm usually ready to begin thinking about what comes next . . . packing away my Christmas things and transforming my Christmas Kitchen back to my ordinary, everyday kitchen. For years my husband used to joke that I put my decorations up on Thanksgiving evening and took them down the morning of December 26.

But I've relaxed a little since then, because I've discovered that the downtime after Christmas, especially the week between Christmas and New Year's Day, can offer a wonderful, peaceful opportunity to ease into the New Year—and it's a perfect time for gathering family, friends, and neighbors and enjoying one another.

After all, people's schedules seem to slow down after Christmas—at least that's true for us. The hectic round of parties and obligations is over. The kids are still out of school. Many people take a few extra days off work. Out-of-town visitors may still be around, and those who traveled for the holidays may be coming home, so now is a good time to get together with them. Plus, the decorations are still beautiful . . . and there may even be some made-ahead goodies still in the pantry and freezer. Besides, New Year's Eve and New Year's Day are right around the corner. So why not take full advantage of the possibilities and plan for some after-Christmas fun?

That's exactly what my large extended family does. We spend Christmas itself at home. (My kids would revolt if we didn't.) But the next week, if we can, we all get in cars and on planes and gather somewhere for an old-fashioned family reunion. It's one of my favorite events of the year, with grandparents, parents, sisters and brothers, cousins, aunts, and uncles. And we almost always find a kitchen somewhere to cook in together.

Even if a reunion isn't practical for your family, I urge you to take advantage of this time to reconnect with people you care about, people you might not have had time to see during the hectic holidays. Think of this as the gentle side of the holidays, and make good use of it.

Then, when New Year's rolls around, take a moment to reflect not only on the year past but also on your Christmas Kitchen experience.

What was the happiest part of the season?

What do you want to do again?

What didn't work—and what worked better than you ever expected?

And what wonderful possibilities will next year bring for you, for those you love, and for your Christmas Kitchen?

Bon Temps Cajun Shrimp

3 quarts water

1 large lemon, sliced

4 pounds unpeeled large fresh shrimp

½ cup extra virgin olive oil

1 tablespoon olive oil

1½ cups canola oil

1/3 cup hot sauce

1 tablespoon minced garlic

1½ teaspoons salt

½ teaspoon ground black pepper

1½ teaspoons Creole seasoning, such as Tony Chachere's

1½ teaspoons dried oregano

1½ teaspoons dried thyme

3 tablespoons minced fresh parsley leaves

3 tablespoons minced fresh basil leaves

Bon temps means "good times" in French, and that's what you'll have with this easy shrimp appetizer, which could also serve as a light supper. Paired with Hoppin' John (page 127) and a green salad, it's a taste of New Orleans that anticipates the upcoming Mardi Gras festivities. If you can find shrimp already cooked and ready to eat, snap them up. Then you can just marinate and enjoy!

Bring the water and lemon to a boil. Add the shrimp and cook 3 to 5 minutes, until the shrimp turn pink. Drain well and rinse with cold water. Chill. Peel and devein the shrimp. Place shrimp in a large, heavy-duty, zippered plastic bag. Combine all the remaining ingredients, stir well, and pour over the shrimp. Seal the bag and marinate in the refrigerator for 8 hours. Drain before serving. Makes 25 appetizer servings

Anne's Healthy Hoppin' John

In the South, black-eyed peas are traditional good-luck New Year's fare. My friend Anne gave me this delicious, easy, and healthy version of a Southern standard recipe with a New Orleans flair. Serve it with Cajun Shrimp, a green salad, and crusty French bread . . . and let the good times roll.

1 cup chopped sweet yellow onion

1 cup chopped bell pepper (I use a mixture of red and green)

1 cup chopped celery

Nonstick cooking spray

Two 14½-ounce cans black-eyed peas

One 14½-ounce can diced tomatoes, with juice

1 cup cooked brown rice

1 cup diced cooked leftover pork or ham, cut into ½-inch pieces

½ cup chicken or vegetable broth

1 teaspoon Cajun seasoning

1 teaspoon bottled hot sauce (optional)

1 tablespoon chopped fresh parsley leaves

Salt and pepper

● ●

In a large skillet or Dutch oven, sauté the onion, bell pepper, and celery with cooking spray until softened. Drain the black-eyed peas and add to the skillet along with the tomatoes, rice, and meat. Add the broth, Cajun seasoning, and hot sauce if desired and cook over medium heat, stirring occasionally, until the liquid is almost evaporated. Stir in the parsley and salt and pepper to taste. Add more Cajun seasoning and/or hot sauce if you like it spicy. Makes 8 generous servings

Confetti Pretzels

One 10-ounce package milk chocolate chips

2 tablespoons vegetable shortening

Candy sprinkles or chopped nuts

30 large thick pretzel sticks (also called pretzel rods)

½ cup white chocolate chips or white almond bark

• • • • • • • • • • • • • •

Place the milk chocolate chips and shortening in a narrow microwave-safe container (such as a tall glass measuring cup) and melt carefully on HIGH, 30 seconds at a time, stirring after each 30 seconds. Place the sprinkles on a plate. Dip each pretzel rod about two thirds of the way up in the chocolate and lay on a waxed paper–lined cookie sheet. When the chocolate is set a little but not hardened, roll the coated rods in the sprinkles. Return to the waxed paper to finish setting or place upright in a glass, chocolate side up, to set completely.

To decorate, melt the white chocolate chips in another container. After pretzels have set, use a fork to sprinkle white chocolate over them. Makes 30 pretzels

These festive snacks are perfect for a party—and so easy! To serve, group them in drinking glasses, confetti side up.

Simple Variations

If desired, carefully melt the caramels from a 14-ounce bag with 2 tablespoons heavy cream. Dip pretzels in the caramel and let set before dipping in the chocolate, then roll in chopped pecans.

If you can find strawberries this time of year, you can use the same basic instructions for making beautiful chocolate-dipped strawberries. Wash and dry the strawberries and chill, then dry again thoroughly with paper towels before dipping them in the chocolate. If you chill the cookie sheet beforehand, the chocolate will be less likely to spread and will be prettier. One package of chocolate will coat a quart of strawberries.

Ambrosia Punch

This beautiful punch is almost a dessert—perfect for your New Year's celebration or almost anytime.

2 quarts orange juice with pulp, chilled

2 cups pineapple juice, chilled

1 cup cream of coconut (not coconut milk), chilled

• •

Combine the orange and pineapple juices, cream of coconut, and apricot nectar in a punch bowl. Add the ice cream in scoops to the punch bowl, then slowly add the ginger ale. Float orange slices in the center of the bowl as a garnish, overlapping one another. Sprinkle toasted coconut over the oranges and top with a cluster of mint leaves. Makes 4 ½ quarts

1 cup apricot nectar, chilled

1 ½ pints vanilla bean ice cream

3 cups ginger ale (I use diet), chilled

2 oranges, thinly sliced

½ cup sweetened flaked coconut, toasted (see page 85)

Mint leaf cluster

Celebrating Your Own Twelve Days of Christmas

❄ *First Day of Christmas*: It's Christmas Day!

❄ *Second Day of Christmas*: Make soup from leftovers (or more turkey enchiladas) and invite the neighbors over.

❄ *Third Day of Christmas*: Volunteer your family to serve an after-Christmas meal at a homeless shelter or youth facility.

❄ *Fourth Day of Christmas*: If you have snow on the ground, invite a group of kids over to play outside (you play, too!). Then warm up with hot chocolate and snacks. This would also be a good time to have a "feed the birds" tree-decorating party (see page 55) with kids.

❄ *Fifth Day of Christmas*: Bake some cookies, go to a nursing home, and sing carols with and for the residents. No one will mind that it's the second, third, or even eleventh day of Christmas.

❄ *Sixth Day of Christmas*: Plan a mini family reunion at your house or a nearby hotel. Look for a hotel that serves breakfast and has a pool for the kids—and a hot tub for you!

❄ *Seventh Day of Christmas*: Host a New Year's Eve skate-a-thon, movie night, or game night for your church's youth group—or just pull out the stops and throw a big New Year's Party for everyone.

❄ *Eighth Day of Christmas*: Gather a few friends on New Year's afternoon or evening, sip some punch, share holiday photos and videos, and talk about the year past and your hopes and dreams for the coming one. If you're ambitious, do some scrapbooking!

❄ *Ninth Day of Christmas*: Have an "undecorating" party—and watch how quickly your home can be back into pre-Christmas shape.

❄ *Tenth Day of Christmas*: Trade some organizational chores with your friends. Make a day of sorting through closets, deciding what to keep, what to toss, what to give away. Then celebrate with a great dinner from your freezer.

❄ *Eleventh Day of Christmas*: If late December or January is considered "off season" where you live, take advantage of the lower rates and enjoy a romantic getaway with your spouse at a nice hotel or bed and breakfast. Make up something decadent in your Christmas Kitchen and take it along.

❄ *Twelfth Day of Christmas*: Be a tourist in your own town. Pack up the family and a lunch and visit a nearby attraction you've never been to. My family always loved to go ice-skating during this time—even when we lived in Dallas!

❄ *Epiphany*: After the Twelve Days of Christmas comes Epiphany, the traditional day for celebrating the arrival of the Wise Men to see Jesus. Throw an Epiphany party with favors of gold coins and scented candles or potpourri (representing frankincense and myrrh). A traditional New Orleans dessert for Epiphany is a King Cake, an iced coffeecake decorated with purple, green, and gold sprinkles—with a plastic trinket baby hidden inside. Whoever gets the baby in their slice gets to throw the next party or bring the cake next year.